THE BEST KEPT SECRETS
IN GOVERNMENT

THE BEST KEPT SECRETS IN GOVERNMENT

How the Clinton Administration Is Reinventing the Way Washington Works

Fourth Report of the
National Performance Review

VICE PRESIDENT
AL GORE

RANDOM HOUSE
NEW YORK

Publisher's Note:

In September, Vice President Al Gore and the National .
Performance Review released a report, entitled "The Best Kept
Secrets in Government." This edition, published by Random House,
reproduces the text of the Government Printing Office Document.

LIBRARY OF CONGRESS CATALOGING-IN-PUBLICATION DATA
National Performance Review (U.S.)
The best kept secrets in government/Vice President Al Gore
p.   cm.
"Fourth report of the National Performance Review."
Includes bibliographic references (p.   ) and index.
ISBN 0-679-77834-9 (alk. paper)
1. Administrative agencies—United States—Management.
2. Government productivity—United States. 3. Decentralization in
government—United States. 4. Deregulation—United States.
5. Interorganizational relations—United States.
I. Gore, Albert, 1948–   . II. Title.
JK421.N34   1996
353.09'1—dc20   96-35174

Random House website address: http: //www.randomhouse.com/
Printed in the United States of America on acid-free paper

Cover design and text design by
Ziga Design

2   4   6   8   9   7   5   3

FIRST EDITION

ACKNOWLEDGMENTS

Putting this little book together was a big job. A flood of facts and narratives came in from all over government, all around the country. Inspiration and skill turned all that into something that we hope is readable and interesting enough to begin to do justice to the reinvention story itself.

Research, data tables, and drafts came from the NPR staff and reinventors working on the report in dozens of federal agencies. I am grateful to all.

The greatest debt of all is due the thousands of federal employees, state and local officials, private citizens, businesses, nonprofits, and other organizations who are changing how government works. Day in and day out, with marvelous creativity, they are finding new ways to do things that make government work better and cost less. They are redefining public service, giving us all a reason for optimism.

CONTENTS

INTRODUCTION

"The era of big government is over."
—BILL CLINTON, 1996 STATE OF THE UNION ADDRESS

When President Clinton said the era of big government is over, he wasn't just making a promise, he was reporting on his progress. The Clinton-Gore Administration has made the federal government smaller by nearly a quarter of a million jobs.[1] This is the largest, swiftest government-wide cut in the history of the United States. It's not just a post-Cold War defense reduction; every department except Justice has become smaller. (See Figure 1.)

The federal government workforce is now the smallest it has been in more than 30 years, going all the way back to the Kennedy Administration. The cuts were long overdue. People had long since grown tired of new government programs initiated each year, with none ever ending. They were tired of stories about senseless sounding government jobs, like the Official Tea-Taster, tired of larger and larger bureaucracies in Washington interfering more and more with their lives. For years, presidential candidates have been promising to make government smaller. But until Bill Clinton, none delivered.

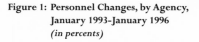

Figure 1: Personnel Changes, by Agency,
January 1993-January 1996
(in percents)

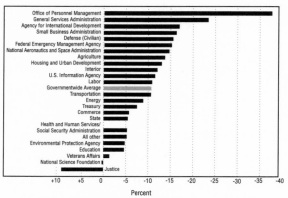

Source: Office of Personnel Management, Monthly Report of Federal Civilian Employment

The workforce cuts are saving lots of money. For fiscal year 1996, the average government worker costs more than $44,000 a year, not including office space and supplies.[2] Cutting a quarter million jobs, therefore, can save well over $10 billion annually. But that's not the half of it. The savings from all the common-sense reforms we have put in place total $118 billion.[*] Put that together with the benefits of our healthy economy, and you'll see that the Clinton-Gore Administration

[*]This total savings figure is derived from three sources. First, $73.4 billion in savings from completed recommendations in the original 1993 NPR report have been realized. Second, another $24 billion in savings have been locked in from additional recommendations in NPR's 1995 report. And third, more than $21.5 billion in savings is attributable to agency reinvention ini-

Figure 2:   **Changes in the Federal Budget Deficit,**
1980-2001

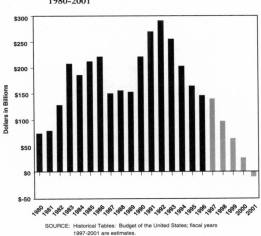

SOURCE: Historical Tables: Budget of the United States; fiscal years
1997-2001 are estimates.

has come up with another one for the record books:
four straight years of deficit cuts, for a stupendous total
reduction of $476 billion.[3] (See Figure 2.)

Even though big cuts in government were long overdue, and even though they are a crucial step in getting
the country out of the red, there is a right way and a
wrong way to cut government. The right way is to
show some consideration for the workers. It is wrong

tiatives beyond the specific recommendations made by NPR. For example, the Federal
Communications Commission realized $20.3 billion by auctioning wireless spectrum licenses,
and the General Services Administration's time out and review of federal construction projects
saved more than $1.2 billion. Other savings from reengineering travel and other administra-
tive processes have not been quantified, but they have saved tens of millions of dollars. In addition, another $5.2 billion in savings is contained in legislation currently pending before Congress.

just to hand out the pink slips and let government employees fend for themselves—workers who have devoted their careers to public service and who have families to support.

We've made the cuts the right way, with layoffs as a last resort. First, we slowed down hiring. The government used to hire well over 100,000 people each year just to replace those who retired or quit. We brought hiring down to fewer than 50,000 a year.[4] We did not stop hiring altogether because many government jobs, such as air traffic controllers, simply must be filled.

Next, we encouraged our current employees to retire or quit by offering them buyout payments. The offers ranged from a few thousand dollars up to $25,000, depending on the workers' salaries and how long they had worked. It was a good deal for the employees and for the taxpayers. Even at $25,000, a buyout costs less than the paperwork and severance pay that goes with a layoff.[5] Nearly 115,000 workers took buyouts.[6]

By slowing down hiring and speeding up retirements, we've managed to limit layoffs to a small proportion of the workforce that left federal service.[7] We are helping those who have been laid off to find jobs with private companies. It's tough, but we're trying. It's all part of making cuts the right way.

Another part of cutting government the right way is to be selective and cut out just the parts we don't need anymore—not the parts we do need. It's wrong to cut activities and services that most people depend on—things like ensuring that our food and water are safe, that our neighborhoods are free from drugs and crime, that tax refunds and social security payments arrive on time. Our plan is ultimately to eliminate jobs we no longer need: jobs in bloated headquarters, excess layers of management, and offices that churn out arcane rules, like the rules that have made government procurement so costly and ridiculous. So far, the personnel reductions have occurred pretty much across the board, because we were trying to avoid layoffs. We'll have to retrain and reassign some people to get them into the right jobs.

A lot of the credit for cutting goes to the very federal workers whose jobs were at stake. For example, it was a procurement specialist, Michellee Edwards, who suggested that we change the law to make small purchases so simple that we no longer need a procurement specialist. Those small purchases used to generate 70 percent of the work in a typical procurement office.[8] Michellee says, "I don't think any government employees would cling to senseless work just to protect their jobs. I certainly wouldn't. For me, it's more

important to keep in mind the bigger picture and promote change where it makes sense. We're all taxpayers too, you know."

This might be surprising, but lots of government
workers think like Michellee. Why else would teams
of personnel specialists have worked so hard to scrap
the 10,000 page Federal Personnel Manual and have
then gone on to cut out much of a typical personnel
office's day-to-day workload by letting employees use
self-serve computer kiosks? Why else would U.S.
Customs Service employees have come up with the
plan that eliminated an entire layer of regional Customs
headquarters that was full of high-paying jobs? Even
Washington's regulation writers are tossing out 16,000
pages of their own creations and removing the bureaucratic jargon from another 31,000 pages.[9] Behind virtually every bit of our successful downsizing and
streamlining are the ideas and the enthusiasm of federal workers. More than anyone, they have the know-
how and the desire to make government cost less. Our
hats are off to them.

A cheaper, smaller government was only half our
goal. President Clinton and I were determined to make
government *work better,* too. You probably haven't read
or heard much about this part of reinvention—although

we never intended it to be a secret—but we've made real progress. The government is beginning to produce more results and less red tape. I'll be the first to say that there is still plenty of room for improvement, but Americans are beginning to see the results in the form of fast, courteous service. Business owners and local government leaders are noticing the change, too, as the federal government becomes more of a partner and less of an adversary. President Clinton and I think it's time everyone knows about these changes—it's time for these secrets to get out.

No one can explain the improvements better than the people who are on the receiving end. So, in the following chapters you'll hear from a front-line federal worker, a homemaker, a business executive, and a mayor. They'll discuss their bad experiences with government in the past. And, frankly, they will tell that there are still some bad things going on. After all, putting common sense into government is a big job, it's still a work in progress, and it probably always will be. But these individuals will talk about a change the likes of which they have never seen before—a change very much for the better.

President Clinton and I are just as proud of making government work better as we are of making it smaller.

It isn't good enough yet, or small enough yet, but we sure have things headed in the right direction. We are rebuilding a government that all Americans can be proud of.

Al Gore

AL GORE

REINVENTION HIGHLIGHTS

Your government is changing dramatically so that it makes sense and serves you better. Here's what the Clinton-Gore Administration is doing to deliver on promises made three years ago:

"THE ERA OF BIG GOVERNMENT IS OVER"

- Government has reduced its workforce by nearly 240,000 as of January 1996. Thirteen of the 14 departments have reduced the size of their workforce; the Justice Department grew because of the Administration's fight against crime and drugs.
- We've cut government the right way by eliminating what you don't need—bloated headquarters, layers of managers, outdated field offices, and ridiculous red tape and rules.
- We've saved and improved the parts you want—Social Security, our National Park system, and other agencies that protect you and your family.
- We're closing nearly 2,000 obsolete field offices and have already eliminated nearly 200 programs and agencies, like the Tea-Tasters Board, the Bureau of Mines, and wool and mohair subsidies.

WE'RE RADICALLY CHANGING GOVERNMENT

Inside the federal government, radical changes are taking place to make it work better and cost nearly $118 billion less than it used to:

- Government workers can now buy $4 staplers because we've cut out the red tape that ran the cost up to $54 in the past.
- We've negotiated better deals for services that the government uses a lot and saved a lot of money in the process, like $3.62 for a three-pound FedEx delivery instead of $27. And as little as 2 cents a minute for long-distance calls instead of 16 cents a minute.
- Government workers are seeing much less of the illogical and bizarre rules and regulations:
  - One-third of the federal workforce used to write rules for and micromanage the other two-thirds. We're getting rid of many of those jobs and are convincing agencies to trust their workers to use their common sense.
  - We're cutting out superfluous layers of managers. We've eliminated nearly 54,000 supervisors—and a few layers.

- In some cases, the Defense Department used to spend more on getting approval for employees to travel than it did on the travel itself. Now they're testing new automated systems that make sense and will save over $100 million a year.
- With new tools like the Line Item Veto and the ability to pursue people who are seriously delinquent in their debts to the federal government, we'll be able to do a better job of safeguarding taxpayer dollars.

WE'RE SERVING PEOPLE BETTER

President Clinton told federal agencies to make customer service to the public equal to the best in business. Over 200 agencies have committed to meeting more than 3,000 standards.

- The Social Security Administration stunned the business world last year by coming in first in an independent survey on the country's best 1-800 telephone service.
- We're changing the Blue Pages in the phone book so if you want a passport, you will look up "passport," without having to know you get it from the State Department.

- Agencies are working together to provide unique services for you:
  - Veterans in New York can access Social Security and Veterans Services with one-stop service;
  - You can go to the "Trading Posts" that the Bureau of Land Management and the Forest Service have set up to get maps, fishing information, and guide permits all in one place and at times that are convenient to you.
  - In Houston, small business owners can go to the U.S. General Store to get information from federal, state, and local governments and even apply for loans.
  - Or just stay home and do government business on the Internet. You can do everything from signing on to the U.S. Business Advisor to get answers to questions, to downloading IRS forms, or filling out a Small Business Administration loan form.

WE'RE CHANGING THE WAY WE TREAT BUSINESSES
President Clinton and Vice President Gore told government regulators to cut obsolete regulations and to start acting like partners. Agencies are eliminating 16,000 pages of regulations and dramatically simplifying another 31,000.

- We're doing it the right way—rewarding companies that cooperate with us. But for those companies that don't work with us to ensure the public's safety and protect our environment, we will apply every penalty and sanction that the law allows.
- The Health Care Finance Administration eliminated the Physician Attestation Form. This ended the filing of 11 million forms each year and saved doctors 200,000 hours of time.
- The Department of Agriculture dropped three million pages of government forms.

We're slashing the regulatory and administrative burden of government on citizens and businesses by nearly $28 billion a year.

WE'RE CHANGING THE WAY WE WORK WITH COMMUNITIES

We're letting states try new ways to reform health care and welfare so they can see what works best by focusing on results, not red tape. President Clinton and Vice President Gore have:

- Created more than 100 federal-local partnerships to focus on the needs of individual communities. These partnerships allow community residents to implement plans to solve what they—not Washington—see as their biggest problems.

- Approved welfare demonstration projects in more than 40 states in the three years before President Clinton signed the welfare reform bill.

- Approved 13 comprehensive Medicaid reform demonstrations in partnerships with states to expand coverage to 2.2 million low-income uninsured Americans.

- Signed agreements with two states—Connecticut and Oregon—to pilot new ways of doing business with less burden, and dramatically streamlined planning and other processes in a range of programs in other states.

THE BEST KEPT SECRETS
IN GOVERNMENT

SECRET ONE: COMMON SENSE HAS COME TO THE FEDERAL GOVERNMENT

"Whatcha got, Bootsie?"

"Coke, looks like about 10 pounds, taped to his chest."

Tommy exchanges high-fives with Bootsie, one of his undercover rovers, as she explains how she picked the unlikely looking drug mule from among the hundreds of incoming passengers on a flight from Colombia. (Don't worry, we won't give away her trade secrets.) A couple more of his rovers quickly team up to check out the smuggler's records, book him, and look for any connections to other passengers or luggage. Within minutes, the troops are back out on the floor, working the next wave of passengers.

Tommy Roland is doing something that any TV cop would envy—running one of the most successful drug-busting operations around. Tommy supervises the inspection team for the U.S. Customs Service at Miami International Airport. "I'm proud of the rovers," he says. "The stuff that they're doing now is defining where Customs is going. I'm thrilled to be a part of that. They use their intuition, their creativity, their imagination on the job. It's really beautiful to watch them. I feel like the coach of some awesome basketball team."

But Tommy says it was not always this much fun. "In the 'olden days,' the whole philosophy of what a Customs inspector was supposed to do and how he was supposed to do it was completely different. First of all, we all wore our uniforms, so we were easy for the smugglers to spot." Today, Tommy is working in jeans and sneakers, and wearing an earring. "We stood in our little enclosures waiting for passengers to come to us with their bags. We didn't know anything about them until we saw the whites of their eyes. We just stood there in our uniforms waiting. A tough way to win a drug war.

"We were looking for needles in haystacks — looking for that nervous passenger, just doing 'behavior analysis.' Everyone who walked off a plane was a suspect. Every suitcase was suspicious. We were unfocused and wasted a lot of time. And at the end of the day, we had dug through a lot of underwear and socks, but hadn't found much dope. What we were exceptionally good at was infuriating the legitimate travelers — hundreds of thousands of honest, decent American citizens and foreign tourists and business executives each year." Passengers sometimes waited in line for over three hours. Occasionally, a fist fight would break out.

Today, cocaine seizures are up by 50 percent. Heroin seizures up by 21 percent.[1] Passengers seldom wait more than a few minutes. This is reinvention.

Tommy says it all started with flowers. "We used to handle cargo the same way we handled passengers — just stabbing in the dark. We knew dope was coming into the country in boxes of flowers. So we probed flower boxes. We used these big metal flower probes and poked away from midnight 'til 8:00 A.M. This was an all night thing, night in and night out. Thirty thousand boxes of flowers came into the airport each night, and we would probe each one once or twice. That's a lot of probe holes. I totally hated Mother's Day and Valentine's Day. Finally, we realized that this was a really stupid way to look for dope — and the flower shippers didn't much like it either. So we sent our own inspectors to South America to look at every single aspect of the whole process.

"We went to the flower farms to see where the flowers were grown. We looked at how the flowers got trucked from the farm to the market, and then to the airport to see how they were staged to get on the plane — who put them on the plane, who hired the people who put them on the plane — and the same on the other end — who took them off the plane and who hired these folks. Looking at the entire process, we saw just how vulnerable a shipment of flowers is all along the way. That's when it hit home. If we were gonna make a dent in the dope, we couldn't do it alone—we had to be partners with the airlines.

"Now the airlines have their own people checking the flowers. Instead of Customs inspectors probing flower boxes here, the boxes are x-rayed before they get on the planes. The airlines have contract security people watching the x-rays. And we video the watchers as a counter-deterrent. They're not our own people so we still check them, but they are our allies, not our enemies. If we had started this earlier, I probably would have saved my shoulder. All that bending over probing flowers wrecked my shoulder."

Partnership with the airlines and shippers has turned out to be the key to success, but according to Tommy, it did not come easy. "Tell the airlines our secrets and have them work together with us to find drugs? Unimaginable. Consider the Immigration Service an ally? No way. Ask the skycaps for their suggestions? Never. Back then everything was a secret and everyone was the enemy. 'If I told you, I'd have to kill you.' That was more like it. Basically, we didn't trust anybody.

"It wasn't just that we didn't trust the folks outside the system. We didn't trust the folks inside the system that much more. A perfect example was all the stupid paperwork we had to fill out. An hour or two before the end of every single shift, we would have to come into the office and fill out a shift report. It seemed like we spent more time writing these reports detailing every single thing we did during the day than we spent looking for dope. It was a real big waste of time and money. And it made me feel like I couldn't be trusted. I really hated that. But things have really changed in the last few years. We got rid of a lot of wasted motion. The guys that work for me don't fill these out anymore. They're paid to look for dope, not to fill out forms.

"I remember lots of hassles I'd have to go through just to do my job. For example, when you're looking through cargo, you might need to drill through a box to see what's inside. But if I wanted to drill, I had to go to a senior inspector who would go to a supervisor who would go to the chief's office where the one drill we had was locked up. Like I wasn't responsible enough to be given the tools to do my job or the authority to make decisions by myself. Now, when inspectors come on board, we give them their own drills. Makes sense to me.

"Even the way the agency was structured sent a loud and clear message about trust. There were just so many layers of bureaucracy to deal with. We used to have regional offices. They were like speed bumps. The guys there had been away from the field so long that you always had to slow down and explain the real world to them. Getting rid of the regions was like a miracle."

What Tommy attributes to a miracle was really the work of a team of employees that Customs Commissioner George Weise chartered to reinvent the U.S. Customs Service. They cut the size of the Washington headquarters by a third, and they eliminated all seven regions and 43 district offices. "In my book, George Weise gets an awful lot of credit," Tommy says. "Not just for cutting out some layers of management, but for really having faith in us down here—trusting us to figure out how to do the job better. It takes some leadership to turn an organization around the way Customs has. He should be proud."

Part of the turn-around came from employing modern tools and techniques. "They assigned me to start looking through the computerized cargo manifests and analyzing information from the airlines," Tommy explains. "This was the first time I had to work with computers looking for dope, and they kinda had to drag me to it kicking and screaming. But in about six weeks, I seized 3,000 pounds of coke using manifest review techniques and targeting.

"Once we realized the power of targeting freight with computer analysis, we wanted to get into pre-analysis of passengers, too. It made sense. If we could get passenger lists when the planes took off, we could start working hours before the plane arrived. We got the majority of the airlines to cooperate. They want to get the dope off their planes. They certainly don't want us seizing their multimillion-dollar 747s. Now, we screen their passenger lists and we know who we're looking for—we go right up to the plane and start working. We don't just stand there in our uniforms waiting for the drugs to come to us. We go out and find it. I hate to use a Washington term, but I guess you'd say we're proactive."

The changes at Miami International Airport are tangible. "These partnerships are changing the whole environment here. There's an energy at this airport that I've never felt in my 22 years here," says Amaury Zuriarrain, deputy director of the Metro-Dade Aviation Department, which runs the airport. "The passengers are noticing the improvements, too."

"It's kind of funny," Tommy adds. "Life is a lot easier for most passengers. They don't have to wait in lines for hours and be treated like suspected criminals. But you know what? Some passengers have written to us that we're not doing our job because the process is so easy for them now. They shouldn't be fooled by that. Just because they don't see me doesn't mean I'm not watching them."

Tommy is dead serious about keeping drugs out of South Florida. "This is where I live. This is where I'm raising my family. And I continually ask myself, 'Is it good to have dope in the schools?' Hell, my kids are in those schools. I don't want dope in my schools. I don't just go to school for Career Day. I go on field trips with these kids. They come to my home. I know every kid's name in my son's fifth grade class. This is my idea of family values.

"It may sound funny, but this experience here at work really has had an effect on my family life. Before, if one of my kids did something wrong, my wife and I would automatically decide how to handle the situation. After all, we're the parents. We're the 'managers' in our family. But we've started to look at things a little differently. We're sharing the decision-making with the boys—asking for their input. They're involved in the decision-making process."

Tommy Roland is a new style "manager" at home and on the job, and it is not just the jeans, sneakers, and earring. He works with energy, creativity, and teamwork, and he produces results. He sums it up simply: "I'm not a bureaucrat. I've got a job to do."

That's obviously the kind of attitude we want in all federal workers. We always have. And most young workers have that attitude when they first sign up. But the government's various systems—procurement, management, and personnel—can sap the energy, creativity, and enthusiasm out of the people who work for the government. Luckily for us, lots of workers all over government are like Tommy. They stick with it anyway because they want so much to do something that really matters—to do something good for the American people. Let's take a look at the systems that de-motivate people, and what the Clinton-Gore Administration has been doing to change things.

Procurement Reform

Most Americans have known for years that government procurement is a mess. But to get a full appreciation, it helps to work here. Before the reinventing government reforms launched in 1993, the typical federal worker was not trusted to buy so much as a $4 stapler for the office. Only trained procurement specialists were allowed to buy things—only a trained specialist could understand the rules—and they would make the buy only if a worker came to them with the forms properly filled out and signed by several bosses up the line—and even then, only if they thought you deserved whatever was requested.

Buying anything associated with a computer was even worse. Federal workers told us about having to get a dozen signatures, and then waiting a year or more to get a simple PC. When it arrived, it was already obsolete, and it cost more than the new, higher-powered models at Circuit City. To cap off their frustration, federal employees would read in the papers, along with the rest of America, that "the procurement system," which did not trust them to buy anything, had gone out and paid $400 for a hammer.

The government's procurement system was enough of a challenge that we decided to double-team it. We got long-time critic of procurement and former Harvard professor of management Steve Kelman to lead some government-wide changes, and brought Colleen Preston in from a Congressional staff to lead reform at the Defense Department. Rather than try to explain all the ins and outs of the regulatory changes backed by the National Performance Review—changes that the Administration has made on its own authority, and changes we have persuaded Congress to enact into law—let's look at some results.

First, results that benefit the entire government and, of course, the taxpayers who foot the bill:

- Last May, we signed a contract with FedEx for overnight package delivery. A three pound package, at retail—$27. For the government, and the tax-payers—$3.62.
- Long distance telephone calls: Someone who shops around can make peak-hour long-distance calls for as low as 16¢ per minute. Starting in October, gov-ernment calls to anyone anywhere in the country will cost about 5¢ per minute. Calls between government agencies are even less, about 2¢ per minute.[2]
- The government used to do over $50 worth of paper-work for every small purchase—even for something like a $4 office stapler—and there are millions of small purchases each year. Now, we have gotten rid of the paperwork and we use special Visa cards. What's special? The average American pays from 12 to 18

percent interest, and a yearly fee of up to $50. The government pays no interest, no annual fee, and we earn cash rebates for paying on time.[3]

- Earlier this year, President Clinton signed a new law and an executive order that fixes one of procurement's biggest nightmares: buying computers and other information technology.[4] Under the President's order, agencies will invest in information technology only when there is a clear payback, and they won't be locked into cumbersome contracts that can't keep up with rapidly changing technology. The idea is to buy a little, test a little, fix a little, and do it quick.

Now for the Defense Department, which accounts for about three-fourths of the federal government's purchases:

- Remember the $400 hammer? How about a $500 telephone—one especially designed for an aircraft carrier. What was so special? It worked even after the ship had sunk. Following changes in the communications system and by challenging every requirement, the Navy determined it could use commercial phones that cost 30 bucks.[5]

- Let's look at socks and underwear (it reminds us of the old days for Customs inspectors). If you were ever a soldier, your GI socks probably fell down because there was no elastic at the top, and they made everything in the washing machine with them turn olive drab. The reinvented Army now issues ordinary, color-fast socks with elastic. The sad-sack socks cost $1.99 a pair—the nice, new ones cost $1.49.
- Concerning underwear, we think this letter speaks for itself:[6]

June 7, 1996

For many years, Jockey International, Inc. declined to bid on government business. We took this position because the solicitations asked us to manufacture a T-shirt to unique government specifications. The solicitations also asked us to provide sensitive pricing data so the government could determine a fair price....

When we saw the latest solicitation for T-shirts we were excited. The government was asking for our standard product, style 9711, without all the headaches of a custom design. Moreover, our current catalog price was the basis to negotiate a fair price. It is with great pleasure that we were able to accept the T-shirt award....

The T-shirt will be made in the USA. The produc-
tion is at our Belzoni, Mississippi plant, an economi-
cally depressed area. This plant was closed in 1993,
but reopened in 1995 on a temporary basis. With a
pick up in business and the award of this military con-
tract we now have 175 employees at this facility. . . .

> *Peter J. Hannes*
> *President, Special Markets Division*
> *Jockey International, Inc.*

Of course, the savings are not all just from socks and
undershirts—the biggest savings come from changes in
buying big-ticket items. When the Pentagon and
Congress agreed to a multi-year purchase and the elim-
ination of detailed military specifications, manufacturers could use more standard commercial parts. As a
result, the price tag on the contract for their new C-17
cargo plane went down by more than $2.7 billion.
Similarly, they saved $2.9 billion on smart munitions,
and over $100 million on the Fire Support Combat Arms
Tactical Trainer.[7] NASA is doing the same kind of thing
and making the same kind of savings on space gear.

In addition to some very important legislative
changes, the procurement system only needed a little
trust (that workers like Tommy Roland won't steal us

blind), some common sense (that Jockey can make decent T-shirts without government instructions), and some shrewd bargaining (just try to find long distance rates as low as 2¢ a minute). That is the heart of the procurement reforms that the National Performance Review recommended in 1993 and that became the basis for three major legislative changes that have been signed by the President: the Federal Acquisition Streamlining Act of 1994, the Federal Acquisition Reform Act of 1996, and the Information Technology Management Reform Act of 1996. President Clinton has gone even further by issuing a variety of directives that enhance and speed the legislative reforms.[8]

Trust, common sense, and shrewd bargaining might not sound like a revolutionary formula to fix government procurement. But added all together, our procurement reforms are expected to save $12.3 billion over five years. Pretty good, huh?

By the way, we are not just buying smarter, we are selling smarter, too. The government actually used to give away the incredibly valuable rights to broadcast on certain frequencies. This included radio, TV, cell phones—you get the picture. Now, the Federal Communications Commission auctions them to the highest bidder. So far, we have taken in $20.3 billion.[9]

Management Systems and Structure

Just a few years ago, the front-line federal workers had more layers of supervisors than they could shake a stick at—as much as they would like to. For example, a nurse in a government hospital would have had to communicate through a reporting chain of a dozen or more bosses before word reached the Cabinet Secretary—and, of course, the Secretary would have to do the same to get an answer back. Remember that party game called "telephone," where a half dozen players lined up and whispered a simple message from one to the next? It invariably came out garbled. Imagine what twice as many players could do. Imagine a dozen or more layers of managers, not to mention their deputies and administrative assistants, transmitting that nurse's good idea about how to save money on, say, sphygmomanometers. Every new idea needed high-level approval.

By the way, that long line of managers was not just waiting to convey the front-line workers' ideas to the top boss. They were busy producing rules and regulations spelling every detail of what front-line workers should and should not do.

Back in 1993, when we began reinventing government, we discovered that one out of every three government employees was part of a network of micro-management and overcontrol. They were headquarters staff, personnel, budget, procurement, audit, finance, or supervisors. One-third of our employees had been assigned to keep the other two-thirds from ever doing anything wrong. They were writing and promulgating internal rules, administering internal rules, and auditing compliance with internal rules. That occupied almost 700,000 workers, who cost tax-payers around $35 billion a year, plus office space and lots of paper.[10] But at least nothing ever went wrong. Right? Wrong!

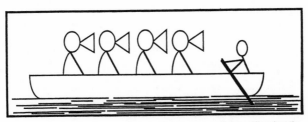

Courtesy of Norm Augustine

Big headquarters and big rule books never have kept the government from making big mistakes. In fact, they often kept front-line workers from doing things right. So we asked agencies to cut layers of supervisors, head-quarters staff, and other management control jobs by 50 percent. Figure 3 shows what they have done so far.

Figure 3:   Streamlining Changes to Date: Fiscal Years 1993-1996

| Agency | Percent Change in the Number of: | | |
	Supervisors	Headquarters Staff	Management Control Positions
Agency for International Development	-3	-14	+5
Agriculture	-21	-15	-11
Commerce	-18	-20	-16
Defense (total)	-16	-10	-8
Air Force	-13	-8	-8
Army	-14	-17	-8
Navy	-19	-7	-8
Defense Agencies	-19	-3	-8
Education	-24	-12	-11
Energy	-53	-27	-16
Environmental Protection Agency	-38	-10	+4
Federal Emergency Management Agency	-20	-22	+17
General Services Administration	-28	-21	-18
Health and Human Services	-29	-15	-11
Housing and Urban Development	-37	-36	-17
Interior	-29	-27	-32
Justice	+4	-5	+9
Labor	-19	-25	-17
National Aeronautics and Space Administration	-40	-34	-16
National Science Foundation	-24	-18	+8
Office of Personnel Management	-53	-65	-41
Small Business Administration	-28	-28	-30
Social Security Administration	-25	-23	-14
State	-8	-7	-1
Transportation	-22	-25	-17
Treasury	-10	+4	+4
United States Information Agency	-22	-15	-17
Veterans Affairs	-28	-19	-6
Average	-20	-14	-9

Note: OMB Circular No. A-11 (1995), sec. 15.4, pp. 47-48, contains the definitions of the job
series included in each of these three categories.

Because we started offering buyouts and putting the
brakes on hiring, the reductions have not been con-
centrated in management control positions to the extent
the National Performance Review recommended. But
11 of the 27 largest agencies are at least halfway to the
goal on supervisors, and eight have cut headquarters
staff by 25 percent or more. In addition, certain bureaus

and agencies within selected departments are also making big progress that is not reflected in their departments' overall figures. Overall, it is fair progress, but we still have a long way to go.

Numbers are not everything. Many bosses are changing the way they do their jobs—encouraging innovation and customer service instead of just making workers toe the line. Many national and regional management organizations are taking on a new role whose primary job is support. Ultimately, we have to bring down the number of people in management jobs and headquarters, but the shift in attitude is every bit as important.

Reinvention Labs

The first thing we did to encourage a change of attitude at headquarters and to move more authority and accountability to the front lines was to create "reinvention laboratories," where front-line workers and managers could try out *their* ideas for a change. Now there are about 250 reinvention labs leading the reinvention revolution. They have been called "islands of innovation in a sea of bureaucracy."[11] The place where Tommy Roland works, Miami International Airport, is a reinvention lab. Here are some other examples:

- The General Services Administration established the first electronic shopping mall for Federal customers, which cut the cost of real estate sales by 50 percent while generating revenue of $73 million.
- The Air Force medical organization prototyped an automated system for maintaining patients' records. The system will save millions of dollars and improve care as it spreads throughout the Defense Department.
- A joint effort between the Defense Contract Audit Agency and the Defense Logistics Agency cut the government's and contractors' overhead expenses by substituting international quality control standards for the government standard. Quality rose, and government costs have fallen by over $150 million so far.
- The Department of Justice's SENTRI project in southwest California uses state-of-the-art technology to reduce the average waiting time to cross the border from 45 minutes to just three minutes for registered travelers. Inspectors now can focus on non-registered, higher-risk travelers.
- A reinvention lab in Anchorage is combining seven separate libraries into a single one-stop shop for information about natural resources. The Department of the Interior is joining forces with state agencies and

the University of Alaska to create a single natural resources library that will eliminate duplication, save money, require less staff, and provide better service to customers.

Personnel Reform

"Filling out the prescribed government job application used to discourage a lot of people. For many, it was their first dose of red tape. It was almost like saying to somebody who wanted to work for the federal government, 'Welcome to the fun house.'"

OFFICE PRESIDENT AL GORE,
IN A SPEECH TO THE OFFICE OF
PERSONNEL MANAGEMENT

In 1883, two years before the first gasoline-powered automobile and six years before the White House had electric lights, the U.S. Civil Service laws were written.[12] Not only is the civil service system old, our first report called it "elaborate, complex, and over-regulated, preventing agencies and their managers, employees, and unions from designing effective and mission-supporting human resource management programs." No one argued with us about that.

We have done what we could to fix it. We have done quite a bit.

Common-Sense Job Applications

We scrapped the Standard Form 171, the ridiculously long job application that said, in so many words, "Welcome to the fun house." Now applicants can send in a regular resume, like regular people do for regular jobs. [13] Even better, the Office of Personnel Management has a toll-free phone service and a World Wide Web site that lets people find out what is available and even apply by phone or fax for many jobs. [14]

Less Red Tape

We junked all but a few parts of the 10,000-page Federal Personnel Manual that specified everything down to the color of personnel folders. We actually hauled it out to a dumpster in a wheel barrow. The death of the manual gave agencies more freedom to tailor things to fit their own operations.

Labor-Management Partnerships

CEOs who had reinvented big corporations told us we could not succeed without a true partnership between management and labor. The President signed an executive order in 1993 establishing the National Partnership Council.[15] Now there are more than 650 partnership councils, and labor-management relations are improving all across government. One of the most successful councils is at the U.S. Mint in Denver, led by Greg Wikberg, president of the local union, and Jack DeBroekert, the manager of the Mint. Since the partnership started, disputes have nearly vanished, litigation costs have dropped by $10 million and, in 1995, they set an all-time record by producing 10.3 billion coins.[16] How's that for a money-making partnership?

Family-Friendly Workplaces

Government workers should have lives, too. Moms and dads need time with the kids, with their own parents, and with each other. So, the Clinton-Gore Administration is encouraging job sharing, part-time work, alternative work schedules, telecommuting from home and from satellite locations, leave banks, and child-and-elder-care services.[17] Top business leaders agree that this approach increases productivity and morale, and reduces lost time.

Performance Appraisals

Every year, everyone who works for the government is to be formally and individually judged by his or her boss. The process can cause tension and is widely viewed as ineffective. Most government work depends on team, not individual, effort. And often, a worker's teammates and customers are better able than the boss to judge that employee's effectiveness. Several agencies are experimenting with different evaluation methods that enhance teamwork and give more influence to the customers. The Department of Education is using a 360-degree appraisal, an evaluation from all directions—the boss, subordinates, colleagues, customers, and suppliers. The other new kind of evaluation is not of the individual, but of the team. It is based on measurable results, and everybody who contributes to the results gets the same grade. Workers are being judged and rewarded in terms of how well their teams achieve measurable results. Several variations of the new systems are being tried, and all have pluses and minuses; the hope is to find better, more productive means of gauging worker performance.

New Civil Service Legislation

Right now, we cannot be as flexible or innovative as we would like to be because the personnel system applies a single set of rules to all federal employees, from patent attorneys to park rangers. No corporation would operate this way. General Electric makes light bulbs, buys and sells mortgage loans, and leases cars. GE does not try to squeeze such a diverse cadre of workers into a single set of personnel rules, and neither should the federal government.

Legislation now moving through Congress will grant agencies more flexibility in administering personnel systems that support their missions, while preserving basic common values like veterans preference and merit. It will allow each agency to set up its own method of rewarding good performance and dealing with poor performance.

Reinforcing Success: The Hammer Award

From the start, Vice President Gore has spotlighted the people and teams that were showing the way to reinvention by giving them a "Hammer Award"—a $6 hammer wrapped in ribbon and mounted with an aluminum frame. It symbolizes the dramatic change from the days when government paid a bit more for hammers. The awards are highly prized, and teams are eager to publicize initiatives that they once would have kept under wraps due to fear of criticism. Nearly 500 Hammer Awards have gone to such teams as:

- the Interior Department team that converted its rules and regulations into "plain English";
- the Transportation team that, along with their California teammates, figured out how to get the Santa Monica Freeway back into operation in record time after the Northridge earthquake; and
- the team from the National Park Service that reduced the review time for construction of park visitor centers and other major projects by over 50 percent.

Several agencies followed the Vice President's lead and encouraged reinvention with special awards. For example, the Deputy Secretary of Veterans Affairs gives the "Scissors Award" to VA employees who have cut red tape.

Franchise Funds

Our government has long opposed private monopolies while creating public ones. A federal manager needing some administrative service—like help from personnel, legal, procurement, financial, or computer specialists—had to go to the departmental monopoly in charge of that service. This approach was thought to offer economies of scale.

Today almost everybody understands that monopolies provide poor services at high costs. So the original

National Performance Review report recommended introducing competition by lifting the requirement that agencies buy supplies from the General Services Administration. GSA's Federal Supply Service gave up its monopoly on office supplies in 1994 and has been competing successfully for government business ever since. Their new motto is "Better, faster, cheaper, or not at all."

The National Performance Review also encouraged agencies to promote competition by establishing "franchise funds."[18] These funds allow selected agencies to offer their common administrative services to other agencies. Congressional approval was obtained in May 1996 for franchise funds in Interior, Treasury, Veterans Affairs, the Environmental Protection Agency, and Commerce. The funds will allow these agencies to sell to other agencies such services as mainframe computing, records storage, personnel and accounting systems, background checks, and travel management.

Our Secret Weapon

Telepathology equipment at the Veterans Hospital in Milwaukee rivals the sick bay on *Star Trek*'s *Enterprise*. But, the real reason the vets get world-class care there is Dr. Bruce Dunn. Dr. Dunn thinks we owe veterans a debt that can never quite be repaid. His research to get vets the best pathology on the planet sets the scales a bit closer to balance.

Helen Wassick went to work part-time in the Morgantown office of the Forest Service in a program that employs seniors at minimum wage. Her office sends out publications all over the country on tree management. Helen prides herself on not giving up on a request until she gets an answer. She says, "I treat people the way I want to be treated." And when the Forest Service started giving comment cards to customers, Helen wrote her own name on the cards. Hundreds of customers told the Forest Service that Helen is the greatest. So now Helen's on the payroll full-time serving customers.

George Hawkins works for EPA in Boston. He used to practice law at Ropes and Gray for more money, and he had a lot less fun. George is the champion in EPA's Boston office for EPA efforts to build partnerships with companies and communities that want to protect the environment. George thinks that this is the future of environmental protection and that building that future is worth doing. He'll tell anyone who will listen. In fact, he wrote 1,000 letters to businesses and towns offering to come and explain the partnership programs.

He got a lot of takers. True to his pledge he has made 150 visits so far this year.

Bruce, Helen, and George all have something in common. A big part of why these people work for government is that they want to make a contribution, to add value, to serve. They brag about it too, over a back fence or at a soccer game. Federal employees haven't done much of that for years. But, in offices where reinvention has begun, the employee teams are inspired by the idea of finding ways to change the system so it serves Americans again.

This motivation is a potent force, a kind of pure energy source for change that has been bottled up. Reinvention turns it loose. The government is filled with good people like Bruce, Helen, and George— and don't forget Tommy Roland. The problem is that for years we have kept these good people trapped in bad systems. We are changing the systems so all our people can devote more of their time, intelligence, and energy to what they signed up for in the first place— serving the people of America.

SECRET TWO: GOVERNMENT IS SERVING PEOPLE BETTER

*"I stumbled from the office dazed and confused,
completely disoriented by what had just happened."*

ELIZABETH CHILDS,
DESCRIBING HER FEELINGS AFTER HAVING CONTACT WITH
THE FEDERAL GOVERNMENT

Beth Childs lives in the shadow of the government—
literally. Her neat, cozy, second-story apartment opens
onto a porch overlooking a federal office building in
Sacramento. They are separated only by a hedge of
white flowering oleander, the kind found in the median
strips of the California freeways. Beth has lived there
for eight years with her husband Bill, a drug and alcohol counselor in a nearby high school, and Sydney, her
junior high–aged daughter. Sydney has recently taken
up playing the flute, following in the footsteps of her
self-taught mother.

"The government is a rude neighbor," Beth com-
plains mildly. "They get out here sometimes on Sunday
mornings around 7:00 making all kinds of noise with
leaf blowers and garbage trucks. But I guess they might
feel the same way about us, considering Fred." Fred is

their gray cat—they also have a calico. "Fred's learned how to open the federal building's electronic doors, and he goes into the cafeteria kitchen. The health inspector caught him in there once. Caused quite a stir." Beth's smile shows that Fred is making up for the Sunday morning noise. Being the government's neighbor is not what made her feel "dazed and confused, completely disoriented" as she wrote in a recent letter. That came from one of the times she visited a government office, when she needed something only the government could supply.

"My twin sister, Tami, just adopted a Russian baby while she and her husband were living in Belgium. The baby's named Amy, and she's absolutely beautiful. Tami had to fill out lots of forms in Russian, Flemish, and French. At the last minute, Tami realized she needed a form in English from INS—the U.S. Immigration and Naturalization Service. It's just a one-page form—a single piece of green paper. I offered to pick the form up at the INS office."

The INS office is in a nondescript concrete and smoked glass building on J Street, one of the main drags in Sacramento. Its address is the only thing printed on the facade of the building, 7-Eleven. But it is no convenience store.

"There was a sign on the wall that said the capacity was 250, but there had to be 500 people in there. I finally figured out I was supposed to take a number. But there were different windows, and there were different numbers and a different number dispenser for each window. One was for forms, but I wasn't sure which one I needed so I took a number for the 'information' window. There was a sign on the window that said, 'Now Serving 143.' My ticket was number 327 and it said right on the ticket there would be a 72-minute wait. So I went out and had some lunch and bought a book. When I got back almost an hour later, the 'Now Serving' sign said 145—I had only advanced by two.

"I decided to skip the 'information' window and took a numbered ticket from the 'forms' window dispenser. It was number 79 and the ticket said I would only have a two-minute wait. Three and a half hours later, I was getting near the window. The reason it was so slow was that clerk kept getting interrupted with questions from people who were dropping appointment forms in a box right by his window. I was impressed by the number of different languages he spoke, and he seemed rude in every one of them. Finally, the clerk had called number 75, so a couple others and I moved up close to the window. Then the lighted sign over the window changed from number 75 to 320! They had switched from 'forms' to 'information.' When we protested, the clerk snapped that he had to do what his supervisor told him, and that he would switch back to forms in 40 minutes.

"With that, he called out number 320, but no one showed. After a second call and no answer, he went to 321 and a young woman stepped up to the window. Well, an elderly woman with 320 had been struggling through the crowd and finally made it. In broken English, she tried to explain that she couldn't get to the window in time. The clerk reprimanded the old woman and refused to help her until she had turned around and apologized to woman number 321. He was really on a power trip.

"I was so mad that I went to a pay-phone in the back of the waiting room to call someone in charge. I got put on hold. I was on hold long enough that the window switched back to dispensing forms. So I hung up and got back in line. When I got to the counter, the clerk said 'Well now, that wasn't so bad, was it?' I had waited a total of five hours. All that time, I could see the forms on the shelf behind the clerk. Why did I have to go through that? He wouldn't even give me two copies of the form in case Tami made a mistake. To get another copy, I would have had to come back another day and wait in line again."

Beth's bad experience at the INS office happened less than a year ago, but even then INS recognized it had problems and was doing something about it. Throughout the country, the agency is beginning to put customers first. For example, they have a new easy way to get forms. Customers can dial 1-800-870-3676 and ask for what they need. In a week or so, the forms come in the mail.

But that's not all. INS has designated two offices — one in Detroit and one in El Paso—as "reinvention labs," where the workers can try out their own new ideas to improve customer service in ways that all INS offices will be using soon. And elsewhere throughout the country, INS's new attitude is catching on. Seven districts are undergoing intensive customer relations training and are running a series of customer focus groups. Incidentally, that same El Paso office recently processed more than 14,000 applications for citizenship within a two-month period; over 10,000 aspirants became new citizens in the El Paso District alone between July 3 and August 30, 1996!

Beth Childs' experience with INS wasn't what left her "dazed and confused, completely disoriented by what had just happened." It was a more recent and more unusual encounter with government that dazed Beth—this one on February 22, 1996. Beth Childs gave her daughter an extra hug as she left for school that day. This time Beth was ready for the long, unpleasant journey ahead. She had made all the plans others make when they go out of town on business for an indefinite stay. Her best friend had agreed to pick up Sydney after school. Not knowing when she would return, Beth wore comfortable, casual clothes and packed her cross-stitching.

To prepare herself psychologically, she closed her eyes and tried to concentrate. She lowered her expectations. She did not expect things to run smoothly or efficiently. Prepared for the humiliation and frustration she had experienced before, Beth drove away to face the government again—this time, the Social Security Administration.

When Beth entered the Social Security office on Fulton Avenue in Sacramento that day, she was shocked. She expected an office filled with long lines of people with screaming children. She wondered if she had gone to the wrong building. The place was quiet. The clerks were smiling. As Beth remembers it, "A strange vortex opened up at the Social Security office and bureaucracy was suspended. I was in shock. I was totally blown away by the service I received. Everybody was just so nice. They almost offered to carry my bags. I felt like they were fanning me with feathers while I filled out this form." Beth was so moved by her experience that she wrote the following letter:

> *Sir / Madam:*
>
> *I had cause to visit your office on February 22, 1996.... I was greeted by an efficient, friendly, help-ful staff in a timely manner and was able to com-plete my business in one visit. I then stumbled from the office dazed and confused, completely disoriented by what had just happened. I wandered the parking lot for a while before regaining my composure and returning home to relay my experience to family and friends. They were spellbound. Thank you for giving us all a new perspective of government agencies and their employees.*

Beth is not the only one who has a new perspective on government. Something similar happened when Beth's twin sister, Tami, brought newly adopted Amy home to the United States this past July. "We got into

Logan Airport in Boston at 5:30 in the evening,"Tami explains. "Amy was still on European time—almost midnight—so she was a bit cranky. When we got to the Immigration counter, we showed the man Amy's Russian passport and her application for citizenship— you know, to get her green card. He told us that the photo on her application was too small. I thought, 'Oh boy, here we go.' But he was so upbeat and friendly. He had a camera in his office, he took Amy's picture, and gave us the right size. Then he noticed that our address on the application was a post office box— we'd been living overseas. He said we'd need a street address to get Amy's green card in the mail. I couldn't remember my parents' ZIP code in Maine, so he asked me their phone number, picked up his phone, and called them. He let me chat a minute to let them know we were safe and sound, got the ZIP code, and sent us merrily on our way. As we left, he called out: 'Your tax dollars at work.'"

They certainly are your dollars, and that certainly is how government should work. Thanks to strong leadership from President Clinton and the hard work of federal employees who have been wanting a chance to do this all along, government is beginning to serve the people better.

President Clinton's Marching Orders

In 1993, President Clinton gave the executive order, and he gave it loud and clear: Every agency that deals with the public should deliver service equal to the best in business. That goal is easy to understand. Government telephone representatives should be as fast and courteous as those at leading mail-order companies. Frontline federal employees should be as eager, able, and happy to serve as the folks at Wal-Mart. The government should serve the people the way America's best companies serve their customers.

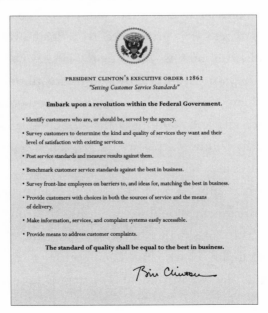

PRESIDENT CLINTON'S EXECUTIVE ORDER 12862
"Setting Customer Service Standards"

Embark upon a revolution within the Federal Government.

• Identify customers who are, or should be, served by the agency.

• Survey customers to determine the kind and quality of services they want and their level of satisfaction with existing services.

• Post service standards and measure results against them.

• Benchmark customer service standards against the best in business.

• Survey front-line employees on barriers to, and ideas for, matching the best in business.

• Provide customers with choices in both the sources of service and the means of delivery.

• Make information, services, and complaint systems easily accessible.

• Provide means to address customer complaints.

The standard of quality shall be equal to the best in business.

Bill Clinton

America's best companies did not get that good overnight, and neither will the government. But we are making progress, and we are measuring our progress the same way top companies do. Their #1 rule in customer service is that you're not making the grade unless the customers say you are. According to letters from some of our customers, we are headed in the right direction:

This is from a recently retired businessman in Mesquite, Texas.——*"Years of less than ideal contact with a host of government agencies had made a 'civil service basher' of me——not particularly kind on my part, but based on experience. And so, on April 8, 1996, I visited the Dallas-Lake June Social Security Office with some trepidation. The waiting room was crowded but I waited only 12 minutes. It's hard to describe what a pleasure that encounter was. Throw out the stereotype of the Civil Service employee. These people were so friendly and helpful that you would have expected that they would be asking favors of us, not the other way around. I can only say that I would hate to be going head to head against you in business. You would win in a walk."*[1]

And this is from a lawyer whose client had some unpaid taxes and a delinquent return.——*"With a few telephone calls (no unending busy signals or being put on indefinite hold) to the Baltimore IRS office, I was able to have an* installment agreement put in place, the levy released by tele-copier, and my client's life able to go on. In 24 years of pri-vate practice, I can't recall an easier resolution of what I had anticipated to be a procedural nightmare."

From a San Diego resident who works in Mexico and used to spend hours waiting in line to come home.—"What a relief it has been, not to worry about long border lines... I'm not sure how to quantify anxiety, stress, and frus-tration levels, but the dedicated commuter lanes have mini-mized these levels significantly. Who knows, maybe I will live longer."[2] Another frequent border crosser notes, "I don't get the stomach aches that I used to."[3]

From an energy analyst who uses Department of Energy technical information—"I would like to thank you especially for the world-class customer service you have given me over the last few years. Employees at Federal Express, Nordstrom's, and Land's End have nothing on you in terms of helpfulness, thoroughness, and responsiveness. As far as I'm concerned, you set the highest standard for excellence."[4]

From a Montana sheriff who had to deal with a derailed train with tank cars leaking deadly chlorine gas; he had to know which way and when the wind would blow.—"Brenda and [the National Weather Service] staff were there for us, in the field, at all hours, and under all conditions. [Their involvement] goes a long way toward dispelling the stereotype *of bespectacled scientists in a windowless room grouped around gauges and radar screens (or a crystal ball ☺)."*[5]

From an inventor in Massachusetts.——*"Joe Cheng [an examiner at the U.S. Patent and Trademark Office] went out of his way to clarify the specifics of patent law. It is people like Mr. Cheng who make it possible for small, independent inventors like myself to survive...."*

From a Detroit police officer who worked security along with the U.S. Secret Service when some international bigwigs visited Motown (movies and TV shows often portray how pleased the local cops are to see the feds show up).——*"In the past, when local and federal agents came together, it would seem like the clash of the titans, but not in this case. It's really hard to put into words, how wonderful and refreshing it was, everyone working together with one common goal ... [and] no finger pointing. Your people are the world's greatest."*[6]

This is part of a letter from a World War II veteran who had gone to a Veterans Affairs clinic four years ago and *"was extremely disappointed by the lack of courtesy and coordination within the clinic."* Recently, he went again. *"What a pleasant surprise! I was impressed by the cleanliness and organization. The clerks were very polite and helpful. Congratulations on a job well done. As my daughter says, we deserve it."*[7]

We agree, you do deserve it—all Americans deserve much better service from government agencies. But it does not come easy. Just listen to what has been going on behind the scenes to make the customers notice a difference.

Who Is the Customer?

We had to start with the basics. Some agencies had never thought in terms of customers before, so the National Performance Review conducted workshops for agencies to figure out who their customers were. In private business it's easy—the customer is the person with the money, the person who might go to your competitor. But most agencies have no competition, and they saw Congress as their source of money. We even had complaints from taxpayers saying they were the government's owners, not its customers. They are right about being the owners, but they are customers, too, like a Ford Motor Company stockholder who buys a Ford.

For some agencies, it was easy to find the customer. The Social Security Administration serves beneficiaries. Veterans Affairs serves vets and their families. But what about agencies that don't usually serve the public directly?

The Department of Education exists to help those trying to learn, their ultimate customer. Yet the

Department doesn't directly operate schools or other learning programs. To get its job done, the Department has to work well with educating organizations, getting them what they need to do their jobs. It's a three party deal—feds, educators, learners—and thinking about that may produce new answers. For example, the Department wants to reach kids with a literacy program. Libraries are looking for new services to attract the public. Kids like pizza. The result is Read*Write*Now, which reached a million kids this past summer.

In the first weeks of summer, Read*Write*Now kits went from the Department to 16,500 libraries. The libraries signed up kids and learning partners—family, teens, seniors, or neighbors. Kids agree to read and write for 30 minutes each day, learn a vocabulary word a day, and meet with the learning partner for help once or twice per week. When the kids finish the challenge, they get a coupon for a personal pan pizza from Pizza Hut, who is a partner in the whole thing.

A different kind of customer relationship exists for regulators—if someone wants to comply with the regulations, treat them right, find out what they want, and give them all the help you can because that will increase the compliance. That's why Richard Hansen, who chairs a transportation committee of Illinois school officials wrote to the Wage and Hour Division of the Department of Labor about Zorka Martinovich and her investigation of an employee complaint. He described her as someone to "work with" rather than someone they have to "deal with." That's why OSHA compliance officers work with S.D. Warren employees who are looking for safety hazards. It's why EPA sits down with Intel to tailor an air permit. And it's why, in public reports, FDA, in an ongoing pilot program, includes company fixes for problems found in FDA inspections. Throughout government, regulators are adding customer-friendly ideas because they get better results than they got with badges and fines. It's a key tool in building partnerships to reach regulatory goals.

When we thought it through, we found that the idea of customers actually worked for all agencies, at least for part of what they do. It's even true for the law-enforcement agencies. The Justice Department is not planning to put mints on pillows in prisons, but they are thinking "customers" when answering requests from other law-enforcement organizations for criminal histories and fingerprints checks. And customer approaches certainly apply to treatment of victims and witnesses.

Ask Customers What They Want

The next step was for agencies to ask the customers what they wanted. Just asking turned out to be harder than one might imagine. In 1980, Congress passed the Paperwork Reduction Act to protect people from having to fill out too many forms.[8] Diligently, the Office of Management and Budget then wrote detailed regulations with stringent requirements that agencies had to satisfy before mailing out any new forms—for example, surveys to find out what their customers wanted. But when the President ordered a new customer service focus, OMB responded and reengineered their system, and now agencies can survey their customers more quickly and easily.

Once agencies began surveying customers, they got some surprises. For example, the Internal Revenue Service had assumed that what people wanted most was to get their tax booklet in the mail as soon as possible after New Year's Eve. But what the customers said they wanted most was little or no contact with the IRS. The Department of Veterans Affairs assumed that vets welcomed long delays in the waiting room so they could swap war stories; their customers told them, "Wrong." (The VA Regional Benefits Office in New York now serves customers so fast that they do not need a waiting room anymore. In fact, they are turning it into a museum of VA memorabilia.) The Federal Emergency Management Agency assumed that disaster victims wanted help to arrive much faster. They were partly right, but the victims FEMA surveyed also said that they wanted someone to take a little time, listen to their worries, and reassure them.

Most people had never even heard of the Pension Benefit Guaranty Corporation (PBGC) or what it does. So PBGC went back to the basics and ran focus groups with customers. When PBGC took over the pension plan from the defunct Cooperweld Steel Company, Rosemary Thomas of PBGC held a town-hall-style meeting. She started by telling 200 worried steelworkers that the agency insured their underfunded pension plan, and that their checks were safe, and how soon the checks would start. That calmed things down right away.

If we've learned anything from reinventing government, it is that the way to get things right is to start by asking customers. By the way, customers like being asked. It was a new experience coming from the government.

Setting Standards

Once customers have said what they want, it is good business to tell them what to expect, the way FedEx promises they will deliver a package by 10:30 the next morning, or Disney World has signs posted along the line for Space Mountain saying how much longer visitors have to wait. Setting customer standards is powerful. They focus on the things that are most important to customers. They also—and this is critical—tell federal employees where to focus. Federal employees need to know what their goal is too. For so long the goal has been not to make mistakes, mistakes as defined by rulebooks too thick to lift. Now the goal is built on the golden rule of customer service, treating people the way you want to be treated.

Making firm promises was new territory for government agencies that were used to hedging. At first, only three agencies—the U.S. Postal Service, the IRS, and the Social Security Administration—were willing to stick their necks out and say how fast or courteous they would be. The next year, after the President's order and more workshops, 150 agencies took the plunge. Now, 214 agencies have published more than 3,000 specific customer service promises. President Clinton and Vice President Gore compiled a book of them, organized it according to type of customer—not agency—and put it on the World Wide Web for all to see.[9]

STANDARDS THAT TOUCH MILLIONS

- *Internal Revenue Service:* tax refunds on complete and accurate paper returns are due in 40 days; 21 days for electronic returns.

- *Social Security Administration:* new and replacement cards mailed within five days; they'll tell customers the Social Security number in one day if it's urgent.

- *Coast Guard:* search and rescue on demand, 24 hours a day, seven days a week.

- *Environmental Protection Agency:* in voluntary programs, publicly recognize the achievements of business partners.

- *Occupational Safety and Health Administration:* inspectors will be respectful and helpful, and focus on the most serious hazards.

- *U.S. Mint:* orders taken 24 hours a day, seven days a week.

- *National Park Service:* Great Smoky Mountains visitor center open every day but Christmas.

- *Bureau of Labor Statistics:* data any way customers want it: from a live person, or by recorded message, fax, microfiche, diskette, tape, Internet, or TDD.

Making promises is risky, but it does force improvement. The U.S. Postal Service promised that local first-class mail would be delivered overnight. [10] They did not make it in key cities. Only 50 percent of the mail was being delivered overnight in New York and Washington; in Chicago, mail burned under bridges. The news media covered it all. But since 1993, on-time delivery in Washington, New York, and Chicago has improved steadily to better than 85 percent by last spring. The national average was up to 90 percent last spring for the first time. [11]

The Convenience of the Customer

After they asked customers what they wanted and set standards, many agencies had to do things differently so they could deliver what they promised. The customer service program is huge. It's customer service teams and customer service representatives and front-line employees in all federal agencies knowing they can truly make a difference and pounding away at the old ways of doing things. It's agency heads sitting down with their customers all over the country to find out what they think. It's federal employees and private sector partners benchmarking best practices in 1-800 service, complaint systems, and more, looking for ideas to improve government's service. It's the President's Management Council aligning planning, budgeting, and operating systems to make sure customer service is mainstream.[12] And we're starting to see results. Enough so that we know that in time we can turn the whole government around.

Here's an example: The Federal Emergency Management Agency had been a national disaster all by itself. Congress was seriously considering scuttling the agency because, when emergencies struck, FEMA was not much help to anyone. Part of the problem was the way FEMA was organized—it had divisions for man-made disasters like riots or nuclear war, and divisions for natural disasters like floods or earthquakes. Each division had people and equipment that could not be used for another division's disaster. FEMA Director James Lee Witt stopped that, reorganizing FEMA into an "all-hazards" team. Other agencies also had to change the way they were organized once they started to concentrate on their customers' needs instead of their own.

In some cases, agencies have organized for the convenience of the customer by banding together. They developed one-stop shops, where the idea is for the government to get together so the customers no longer have to wander around. For example, Houston, Boston,

Kansas City, and Atlanta now have a "U.S. General Store" offering almost any service from the federal government in one place, with state and local governments there, too. SBA is there for loans and advice. The IRS is there for help with tax questions. The agencies that don't have people in the stores have set up hot-lines to answer questions right away. This way, for example, EPA advice is easy to get. One-stop.

"Trading Post" meant one-stop for everything on the American frontier. Now the Bureau of Land Management and the Forest Service, who often manage adjoining lands, are teaming up in new Trading Posts. Customers told the agencies it didn't make much sense for people to make two stops for maps, fishing information, woodcutting fees, and guide permits. So the agencies are moving in together. In Canon City, Colorado, they got the Colorado Division of Wildlife to join them, giving outdoor enthusiasts a better deal still.

And to gather firewood in Oregon, citizens can stop by the local convenience store, where they buy milk and bread, to buy a permit for federal wood, whether it grows in an Agriculture Department National Forest or a Bureau of Land Management area. We figured it out so the taxpayer doesn't have to.

There is no doubt that one-stop works for customers. Maybe that is how government services should have been put together in the first place.

Phones

Workers need good equipment to give good service. Let's stick with FEMA as the example: FEMA's main equipment used to be tents and tons of paper. After a flood, FEMA would set up a tent on dry ground and all the victims would have to go there to fill out forms. FEMA inspectors would stop by the tent, pick up a batch of forms, slog out to the damaged houses to check them out, then slog back to the tent to exchange those forms for the next batch. To give better service, they needed better tools, and they got them. Now, flood victims can call a toll-free number to apply for aid, and inspectors have hand-held computers with modems that receive claims and transmit their evaluations without any slogging. Many other agencies needed and got modern equipment to give better service, too.

Telephones are a top priority in customer service all across the government because more Americans contact the government by phone than any other way. The attention is producing better service.

Last year the people at the Social Security Administration were judged the best in the business at handling
calls. An independent survey by Dalbar, Inc. picked SSA
as the best toll-free telephone service, compared to several top private sector firms. SSA beat Xerox, Southwest
Airlines, L.L. Bean, and Disney.[13] But SSA wasn't satis-
fied—it took too long to reach an operator. The service
was world-class, but the access was not. This year, Social
Security transferred staff to the call centers, converted
data centers to handle calls, put in technology so that
all claims representatives could handle overflow calls on
the busiest days, and installed a 24-hour automated system for frequently asked questions. Now, less than half
as many callers get busy signals, and 90 percent of all
calls go through in less than five minutes.

FEMA and Social Security are not the only ones who
see phones as the key to better service:

- The Food Safety and Inspection Service has a 24-hour,
  seven-day-a-week, toll-free number with safety tips
  and information on recalls of meat and poultry.

- The Food and Drug Administration has a 24-hour
  phone line and a World Wide Web site with information on food, drugs, and cosmetics.

- Starting in November, travelers worried that a new
  passport will not arrive before their flight leaves can

dial the Passport Service's new 1-900 number and find out the status of their application.

- The Consumer Product Safety Commission's toll-free hotline runs around the clock. Callers can report hazards or hear about recent product recalls. For auto safety information, the Commission will transfer callers to the National Highway Traffic Safety Administration's hotline.

- The Immigration and Naturalization Service now has a toll-free number for forms (so no one has to suffer what Beth Childs did). They also have a gizmo that employers can attach to their phones to call the INS computer and verify the legal status of job hunters.

- IRS is always on the phone. The TeleTax system is available to provide recorded information to all taxpayers. And this year, three million taxpayers called in and filed their returns by touch-tone phone using a pilot program called TeleFile. TeleFile checked their math and sent their refunds to them within three weeks.

THAT NUMBER, PLEASE

Auto Safety Information   1-800-424-9393

Consumer Product Recall Notices   1-800-638-CPSC

Export Assistance for Business   1-800-USA-TRADE

Immigration and Naturalization Forms	1-800-755-0777
Meat and Poultry Safety Tips	1-800-535-4555
Social Security Information	1-800-772-1213
Taxes, Recorded Information	1-800-TAX-4477

Number, Please

With the government providing more and more services over the phone, what is the phone number? Try 411—information. Ask the operator about a government service, like getting a passport. The information operators hate calls like these because, like the rest of us, all they have to work with are the government listings in the phone book. The low-tech puzzle that must be solved before reaching the high-tech government is the "blue pages."

The blue pages are not like the yellow pages. Yellow pages list things and services. Blue pages list names of organizations. The information operator would have to know that the question about passports would be answered by the State Department (listed under "S").

We are fixing the blue pages. The General Services Administration handles phone services for the government, but each agency creates its own listings in each phone book around the country, so changing the blue pages is a big coordination job. Nonetheless, as a start, GSA and the agencies have promised to have new blue pages in at least five cities reaching 11 million people this fall.[14] Soon, callers wanting a passport will look under "P" for passport.

Computers

Some technologies have just been waiting to be discovered by the government. The corner ATM machines and supermarket checkout stands used by most Americans already hold the technology needed for a national Electronic Benefits Transfer system. This grand reinvention plan, announced in 1994, will deliver food stamps, social security, veteran, and local assistance payments using a single debit card for each beneficiary. By 1999, about 25 million Americans will be using the card to get benefits totaling $110 billion per year, instead of getting checks or food stamps.

All states are planning Electronic Benefit Transfer systems. Thirteen are already delivering some benefits this way, with about 3.5 million citizens using the card. Checks are no longer mailed or carried around so there is less chance of theft. Electronic records make it easier to spot fraud. When the program is completely up and running, it will save about $230 million per year in administrative costs.[15]

Since April of 1996, a service to order your personal benefits estimate from the Social Security Administration, called PEBES, has been available via the information superhighway to the World Wide Web site.[16] The statement of expected retirement and other benefits has been around for years, but you had to get the paper form, fill it out, and mail it in. This all happens now from your computer screen in about five minutes.

The Web site provides a place for people to offer comments. Reactions are overwhelmingly positive, about how it is easy to use and convenient. For example, Ralph Sabelhaus said he meant to get the form for months and never got around to it. But the best compliment comes from Reggie Lewis, who visited the Web site and left this message, "This is too easy—is this a trick or something?"

The World Wide Web and technology are not for everyone—not yet. However, for more and more Americans technology plays a central role in their lives. It brings them new options, like how to pay for groceries. It brings convenience, like making a call from the car. It gives them control over their own lives, like booking travel reservations from their computer on their desk at midnight. In a world where so much is out of our personal control, anything that lets us drive is welcome. In addition, many visitors to the government's new Web pages talk about the feeling of once again being in touch with their government.

Inside government, the technology lets us get and share information more quickly. We can push it out to the front lines, where change is encountered first and customers want decisions now. We can collect information overnight from everywhere and get it to managers so they can react to changing needs. Technology lets us think of brand new ways to do things, one-stop ways, paperless ways, in flatter organizations, with lots of people working on the same thing at the same time, what computer techno-weenies call massive parallel processing. In short, technology is the great enabler for reinventing government.

But, but, but our idea is not to force people to use technology. Our customers are being given choices. They can come in, call up, fax an order, or go by Internet. They can get a tax check by mail or direct deposit. Often the technology will be invisible, behind the wizard's curtain helping the government employee who serves them.

When government's customers choose technology options, the burden on other services that depend directly on face-to-face, or voice-to-voice contact goes down. That means better service for those still choosing the old routes. For those choosing new routes service should be better too. The technology solutions are going to be faster, with fewer steps in front of and behind the curtain, and they are going to be cheaper. And cheaper is the critical word if we are to improve customer service in a balanced budget world.

Social Security's PEBES project is not a lone government success on the Internet. At the Department of Agriculture, they put the first ever standardized data base for plant species on-line. A niche product? Not exactly. There are 200,000 requests per month at the Web site, which was built by the Natural Resources Conservation Service for users that include scientists, teachers, and state and federal government agencies.

The most used home page in government, and maybe anywhere, belongs to the IRS. It looks and reads more like small town newspaper than a part of government. It answers frequently asked questions, goes over 148 tax topics, and explains recent regulations, trying to be as easy to understand as possible. It also provides access to IRS forms, publications, and instructions. From January to June 1996, there have been 60 million electronic accesses on the home page. Just on April 15, taxpayers downloaded 104,000 files. The next day there was a run on the forms for late filing.

Students and teachers have been enjoying "Ask-a-Geologist," the U.S. Geological Survey's new Internet service.[17] Sorry, kids, they'll answer questions but they won't write your reports.

Existing technologies are getting new uses all over government. John Conroy is a realtor in Naples, Florida, and back in May he had a little problem. He needed 75 years' worth of Consumer Price Index data to calculate the value of a property he was working on. It was late in the afternoon, but being an optimist, John called the fax-on-demand hotline at the Bureau of Labor Statistics.[18] Zap, he got a catalogue, called in an order, was surprised to find that he didn't seem to be bothering the people at the Bureau, and got his data by 10:37 the next morning. "Refreshing change," says John.

Some agencies are writing neat software packages and giving them to customers. HUD has an amazing little package that draws a city map and, block by block, shows where in the city all the HUD grant moneys are being spent.[19] Among other things, cities and interest groups use the software to play "what if" with alternative plans to use the money.

The Bond Wizard responds to requests from holders of U.S. Savings Bonds for a simple way to calculate the redemption value of their bonds. The Wizard is from the Bureau of the Public Debt and is available as a diskette or on-line to Internet users.[20]

For over a decade VA has been taking shots for using outdated technology in medical care for vets. But in Milwaukee, VA is setting medical standards for a remote diagnosis technique that is a breakthrough in the field of telemedicine. With this technique, expert pathologists in Milwaukee use a high-speed data link and microscope robotics to assist doctors diagnosing patients 218 miles away in Iron Mountain, Michigan. The technology gives results as good as those the pathologists get in Milwaukee. The obvious payoff is better care for vets through wider access to experts. At the same time, VA keeps the lid on physician costs by making better use of specialists.

Just a Little Common Sense

So much of what is happening to improve customer service comes from simply giving federal employees the goal of serving customers and the freedom to do it. Often their ideas are low-cost or money-saving testimonials to the return of common sense.

One morning, Hugh Doran, Director of the VA Medical Center in Kansas City, drove to work and parked in his reserved space in a lot near the clinic entrance—a lot used only by VA employees. That morning, Director Doran decided to charge a diverse group of employees, patients, and service officers with evaluating the overall parking situation. The group recommended converting the existing reserved lot to patient parking. Now, Doran parks with all his employees and walks through the new patient parking lot next to the building.

A few months later, Doran and his team were discussing the need for space to accommodate primary care patients. They realized that the most convenient place for primary care was on the first floor, and Doran decided to move the director's and administrative offices out of their prime first-floor space. Very soon, they were relocated to the fifth floor, and the first floor was converted to primary care facilities. Today that area is dedicated to serving over 3,500 veterans.

Moving administration around to make life better for veterans is a trend at VA. They did it in Lebanon, Pennsylvania, and Wichita, Kansas. In Boston, Pittsburgh, Philadelphia, and Biloxi, they moved to make first-floor space available for easy-to-reach facilities devoted to women's needs.

Common-sense changes save some money, too. Gail Mirsky works with victims and witnesses at the Justice Department. She noticed that witnesses and victims who needed to travel for the Justice Department had to book their own travel. After their trips they sent in travel vouchers and waited to be paid. Gail figured that, instead, the government could set up an account with a travel agent, where travel could be booked at the government's volume discount and paid directly, so witnesses could avoid being out of pocket for expenses. This works like a charm and also saved the government about $150,000 in the first 15 months.

Forest Service employees are also putting their money-making, common-sense ideas to work. Did you ever wonder what happens to all those big trees cut each year from city streets and parks? Most end up in landfills or, at best, in a compost pile or firewood stack. In New Jersey, the Forest Service showed a couple of towns how to cut the trees for sawmill use, resulting in new wood products, jobs, and income for the cities.

Training

Finally, there is training for all the front-line workers who actually see and talk to customers. All the clerks waiting at the counters. All the operators poised for your call. And training for the managers, too. They have to learn what the best companies in business know—that employee satisfaction is the key to customer satisfaction. Some of the nation's top experts in customer service have volunteered their time to teach at a couple dozen customer service workshops for federal workers.

A new organization, formed by cutting and combining three old agencies in the U.S. Department of Agriculture, hadn't settled on a name for their new operation, but they had figured out that they existed to serve customers, the farmers, and rural communities. So their first goal was to train everyone—all 12,000 employees—in customer service. This, they said, was the only sensible thing to do. For them, the National Performance Review's customer service program was not just another program. For them, it is *the* program.

They have a name now. It's "USDA Rural Development." The first round of training is done, and if you talk to the employees, they'll tell you it made a big difference. They learned things that let them understand what customers are going through, and they know they are doing a better job. The nice fan mail they are getting says they are right.

The trick was to pull together all the new awareness of who the customer is and what the customer wants, all the capability of the new organization and the new equipment, and all the common sense and caring that federal workers bring to their jobs. The reorganized FEMA, for example, has done exactly that. With the new toll-free phone service and their inspectors using hand-held computers, FEMA's "all-hazards" teams can move a lot faster, get plenty of resources on the job quickly, and cover more territory in less time. But they had to be trained to spend some of that extra time just listening to people's troubles and reassuring them, like the customers said they wanted.

It's a big job to get an entire government turned around from focusing on red tape to focusing on results that customers want. The Clinton-Gore Administration is leading the way, and we think we're getting there. But the only opinion that really counts is the customer's:

> *Dear FEMA,*
>
> *The morning of August 9th [1995] completely changed our lives. Vermilion, Ohio, had five inches of rain in under one hour. Our basement began to fill with water and when the pumps failed we knew we were in for some problems. The basement windows*

burst in with incredible force and within an hour and a half we had eight feet of water in the basement and five feet on our first floor. We were completely helpless, and had just enough time to rush our two small children to safety. We lost nearly everything we owned. I cannot begin to explain the feeling of watching the water come up in the doors and windows. Frantically we tried to move things but the water just came in too fast. It was truly terrifying and so incredibly sad that everything we worked so hard for was now five feet under water. It is a feeling that will never ever leave me. We were at that moment without a place to live, no clothes other than what we had on, and a realization that we had no flood insurance (we were not in a flood plain area). It was very devastating.

Then the Red Cross and FEMA arrived. I must tell you that the people working for you are some of the nicest, most caring individuals we have ever met. They were so willing to do anything in their power to help. They were so wonderful, each and every one of them. They treated each person that walked through the door as if they were their own family. . . . They were so unbelievably organized, whatever they said they would do—it was done. They had answers and got *right back with us. They were always right on time and were so helpful.*

Thanks to you, and only you, we were able to get back on our feet. Our children were truly traumatized by the flood and you enabled us to get things back to normal, and get into a home again. We owe you and the President more thanks than we can ever express. If I had the chance to tell the President one thing it would be that FEMA is the answer to prayers.

In closing there is nothing I could say as to how FEMA could work better to help its customers...

Sincerely,

David and Kelly Bodde, Jordan and David [21]

SECRET THREE: GOVERNMENT IS IN PARTNERSHIP WITH BUSINESS

All Regulators Will:

- ✓ Cut obsolete regulations
- ✓ Reward results, not red tape
- ✓ Get out of Washington—create grass roots partnerships
- ✓ Negotiate, don't dictate

Bill Clinton *Al Gore*

February 22, 1995

The relationship goes way back. In the early 1800s, the U.S. government drew on the resources of Saint Simons Island off the southern coast of Georgia—its tough live oaks made the sides of the frigate USS *Constitution* withstand cannonballs like iron. Almost a hundred and fifty years after Saint Simons made "Old Ironsides" famous, a group of island entrepreneurs turned the tables and drew on the resources of the U.S. military—they leased large freezers from the local Navy base that was closing and became SeaPak, the nation's first commercial producer of breaded shrimp. Today, half the nation's retail frozen breaded shrimp, millions of pounds of breaded fish filets, onion rings, French toast sticks and cheese sticks come from Rich-SeaPak, whose corporate offices are still on Saint Simons Island.[1] The long relationship with the government has had its ups and downs.

"The seafood industry traditionally had very adversarial dealings with the FDA" (Food and Drug Administration), says Ray Jones, SeaPak's corporate director of quality assurance and regulatory affairs. "In the early days, it was all small, independent producers—basically fishermen—who didn't want anything to do with the government. It was a matter of getting away with whatever you could. So when bigger companies like SeaPak started to be formed, the residue of that adversarial relationship was still around.

"When I came here nine years ago, our lawyers were telling us, 'Don't talk to them, don't give them anything.' We could do that legally. The law says that we have to let FDA come into the plant and go anywhere they want. But, we don't have to give them our production records or consumer complaints or let them take pictures. So we didn't.

"One of the things the food industry has always feared is giving FDA access to customer complaints. Most customers give us good, legitimate feedback on what they think about our product, but there are some complaints that we get that may not be legitimate—such as where a customer alleges they found something in a package of shrimp or fish. We were afraid that FDA might mis-interpret or overreact to the complaints, so we chose not to let FDA see them. They would come in, ask for the customer complaint file or some other records, we'd refuse, and things would go downhill from there.

"The thing FDA did that hurt us the most was taking samples of our product. They would take the samples and send them off for analysis. Sometimes it could take weeks to get the results back. We were not required to hold the product off the market until the testing was finished, but we almost always did. So sometimes we might have to hold two or three days production until we got the results back. Even if we were sure the prod-uct was in compliance, we did not want to risk the pos-sibility that FDA might find a problem and then we would have to recall the product if we had already shipped it. So we would hold the product and wait.

"Keep in mind that, all this time, SeaPak was running a clean operation. We're very careful about the whole-someness of our product. Not just when the FDA shows up, but all the time. The only thing that was coming between us and them was a bad attitude. Ours, at least as much as theirs.

"In 1992, I sat down with our CEO, Frank Holas, and looked at our latest inspection report. We agreed it was

ridiculous. We had set high standards of quality for our-
selves—that's what our customers demanded. We
exceeded the regulatory requirements as we under-
stood them. So why were we always at odds with the
FDA? We were as ethical or more ethical than anybody
else we knew in the business. FDA should have had us
up on a pedestal as an example. But it was the pits.

"At any rate, we got tired of the old adversarial relationship at just about the same time Clinton and Gore
started pushing the agencies to try partnership. It all
worked together in parallel. We called the FDA and
said we'd like to talk. So we went up to Atlanta (FDA's
regional office) and all the players were there—including our local inspector from Savannah. We asked them
what we had to do to change things. They said, 'How
about knocking off all these refusals when we ask for
files and records.' We said we would if they would work
with us to solve any minor violations they might find.
We wouldn't expect them to ignore real safety issues—
we didn't think we had any of those anyway—but we
didn't want them to punish us for minor paperwork
problems we could quickly fix, or force us to recall a
product due to an obviously phony customer complaint.

"Well, no more than 30 days after we got back from
Atlanta, they came to inspect us. I guess they wondered

if we were for real. We let them see everything they asked to see. Our lawyer almost had a heart attack. The key to this whole approach is one-to-one relationships. I told their inspector, 'Look, my job is on the line here. We got to have trust on both sides.' We came out of that with the best inspection report we ever had. And they've been back three times to inspect us since and it keeps getting better."

All the time SeaPak was changing its combative attitude, FDA was changing, too. FDA's field investigators traditionally have been rewarded for detecting violations and levying fines. But FDA has begun to emphasize public safety over disciplinary action. This reorientation encourages more open communication between FDA and industry. For example, FDA recently inspected a food-canning operation and found a malfunction in the sealing equipment, a serious problem that could have led to a botulism outbreak. Instead of launching a lengthy, formal enforcement action, FDA inspectors quickly recommended to the cannery owners that they destroy all cans in the lot and repair the sealing equipment. They agreed and the problem was resolved immediately. This on-the-spot teamwork saved the agency and the company thousands of dollars and immediately protected consumers from dangerous products. That's the way of the future for FDA.

What does Ray Jones at SeaPak see in the future? One word: "HACCP." Ray's not clearing a fish bone. He's talking about the Administration's new scientific way to insure the safety of our food.

"It means 'Hazard Analysis Critical Control Point,' and basically, it's the same method the Japanese used to beat the pants off our auto industry in the seventies and eighties. You build in quality all along the line—don't wait 'til the end and just spot check the product. It's a much better way to ensure food safety. In simple terms for the seafood industry, it means making sure cooked fish stays hot enough long enough that no germs could possibly still be alive—and for raw fish, that it stays cold enough until you're ready to cook it, so that no germs can grow. The FDA will be looking at our production control records to make sure we get things hot enough, or keep things cold enough. They'll check the product randomly to verify the other checks. But the quality's built in. We think it's great. In fact, I'm training to become a certi-fied HACCP instructor so I can teach our suppliers and even our competitors the new techniques."

Ray explains why SeaPak welcomes a new regulation that gives FDA access to production records. "We think it will improve the consumer's confidence in seafood. Seafood's taken a bad rap because of things like raw oysters. But shrimp and breaded fish filets are the safest foods you'll ever eat. This new scientific inspection will boost confidence. Five years ago, we would have been worried about letting more government in the door. But we're not afraid of that anymore. We trust each other. We have the same goal—top quality food for our customers. We're partners."

Forming Partnerships

Can federal regulators really be partners with industry? We are not naive. We know that not everyone is going to play by the rules. There will still be bad actors who will not comply. For them, we reserve every penalty and sanction that the law allows. And because regulatory time and effort is no longer being wasted on the good guys, agencies can better focus their attention on the few cheaters.

But experience shows that the vast majority do play by the rules—if they can figure them out, that is. In dealing with that majority who want to do the right thing, partnership can achieve very good results. If we agree on the goals, allow room for innovation, and help each other all we can, that will increase compliance.

With that in mind, we called together all of the top regulators in Washington for repeated meetings to reach consensus on a new approach—a way to make the rules make sense, a way to bring the vast majority of businesses into compliance, a way that works better and costs less.

The Environment

The Environmental Protection Agency (EPA) used to focus on cleaning up pollution. Now the idea is to prevent pollution, and to use partnership as a mainstream approach. EPA has found that when they let companies volunteer to cut pollution without the government dictating how they had to do it, thousands of companies jumped at the chance.

Since 1992, EPA has more than tripled membership in its "Partners for the Environment" program, with over 7,100 companies now participating.[2] One of these partnerships was forged by EPA's Regional Administrator in Boston, John DeVillars, with The Gillette Company, which has a good track record of compliance. Under a program DeVillars calls "Star Track," an independent firm audits Gillette's compliance with environmental regulations, and makes the audit reports public. Gillette pays the cost of the audit and gets amnesty to fix non-criminal violations without being fined. EPA makes no other inspections, and Gillette makes no other reports.

In March 1995, President Clinton offered this additional challenge to companies: "If you can meet even higher environmental performance standards, we will provide flexibility and cut red tape so you can find the cheapest, most efficient way to do it." Today, EPA's Project XL—for "excellence and leadership"—has more than a dozen projects with industries, states, and cities getting under way around the country.

Altogether, EPA's partners removed from circulation an estimated 4 billion pounds of planetary poisons just in the last year.[3] Since the companies did it their way, instead of Washington's way, they saved $360 million in the process. It is such a clear winner that EPA expects to sign up 10,000 new partners in the next four years.[4]

Figure 4: Number of Participants in EPA Partnership Programs

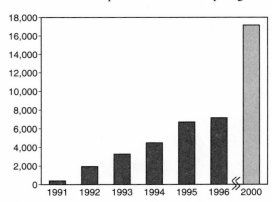

SOURCE: Unpublished data from the Environmental Protection Agency; data for year 2000 is an estimate.

Medicine

FDA has been cultivating partners in the drug industry, too. Their new goal is to "make safe and effective drugs available" to Americans, whether from the most conventional processes or from the newest biotechnology. FDA will never compromise on safety, but that is not stopping them from cutting out bureaucracy. Scios, Inc., a northern California pharmaceutical manufacturer, recently wrote the agency thanking it for its new approach, in which inspectors work with companies to identify and correct problems, rather than just issue reports of deviations. [5] Citing a recent visit to its facility by an FDA inspector, a company vice president remarked on the frustrating history of industry relations with the agency, noting that, "… since the late 1980s, relations between FDA and its regulated industries have been on a steady and disheartening decline." However, the new approach taken by the FDA inspection team was a refreshing change: "Our goal is to get safe and effective therapies on the market as soon as possible; you've contributed to this effort," the executive states in commenting on the new and welcome change in the FDA.

FDA has been working in partnership with industry researchers to create safe, effective new drugs against cancer and other killers, and to market them fast. For example, they worked with Merck & Co., Inc., to make an important new tool in the fight against HIV/AIDS available faster. Knowing that scientists at Merck were nearing a breakthrough on a new drug to treat HIV/AIDS, the FDA set up advance teams for regulatory review and manufacturing inspection to reduce delays in the approval process. In particular, the Baltimore district office of FDA worked with Merck's Elkton, Virginia, facility to integrate the review process with the construction of the new manufacturing plant and validation of the manufacturing process. As a result, Crixivan, one of a new class of protease inhibitors offering significant new treatment in the fight against HIV/AIDS, was cleared for the market in 42 days, the fastest ever approval of a new drug by the FDA.

Worker Safety

When workers contact the Occupational Safety and Health Administration, they are usually worried about life and limb in the place where they go to make a living every day. The "old" OSHA would send off letters to the employers, some of whom didn't have a clue they had a problem. In the meantime, the worker waited up to a month for action. Not anymore. Now OSHA calls the employer—usually within 24 hours—and works out a plan to fix the hazard. The fax speeds documents back and forth. It's common now for hazards to be resolved in a week rather than a month.

Industry leaders like this "new" OSHA. The new OSHA emphasizes increased partnership with companies, and it's paying off. Joe Dear, Assistant Secretary of Labor for Occupational Safety and Health set up a team of experts from OSHA's compliance officers, managers, union representatives, and support staff all over the country. He asked them to design a new way to protect American workers. This "design team" created an approach that puts more stock in results than in rulebooks, and they're using it in field offices nationwide. The new way includes not only rapid response to worker complaints but also partnership with companies to work on long-range prevention of health and safety hazards.

One partnership is with Horizon Steel Erectors Company. Horizon teamed up with OSHA's Atlanta office, Argonaut Insurance Company, and the Department of Defense. Horizon, building a Defense facility in Florida, said that each worker would use fall protection and that supervisors would enforce this commitment. In the first 90 days, Horizon had a 96 percent reduction in accident costs per work-hour—from

$4.26 to 18 cents. In six months, the total cost of workers compensation claims fell from more than $1 million to $13,200.

There's more. Horizon President Ken Sanders told OSHA that three lives were saved in three separate falls because the workers were wearing fall protection gear. Now Horizon Safety Director John Paulk travels at company expense to tell others about the new OSHA.

Even though we believe the partnership approach has a big payoff, we will never lose sight of the government's basic responsibilities and will never give up the ability to enforce the rules. In the Maine 200 program, OSHA told the 200 most hazardous companies in Maine that, if they would run good safety programs, traditional inspections would be a low priority. Worker safety soared, and OSHA is establishing similar programs nationwide. When one of the Maine 200 companies reneged on its commitment and subjected its employees to extremely unsafe and unsanitary conditions, OSHA stepped in quickly, cited them for dozens of violations, and fined the company $3.6 million.

Pensions

The departments of Labor and Treasury are simplifying the rules and regulations that ensure company pension plans are financially secure. Under the new rules, companies file less paper and do less mind-numbing math. More small businesses will be able to start pension plans covering more workers. And the workers can feel more secure than ever that their money will be there when they reach retirement age.

In August, President Clinton signed legislation to provide better pension coverage and security for workers. The new law expands opportunities to save for retirement. It improves the protection of pensions and removes obstacles facing many workers who want to bring their retirement savings with them when they change jobs. It also simplifies the pension rules to make it easier for small businesses to set up and run pension plans. Ten million workers in small businesses could benefit from the new, simplified 401(k)-type plan—no red tape, just a simple form.

Health Care

The Health Care Financing Administration is shifting from red tape to results so doctors and hospitals can focus more time and attention on their patients. For example, doctors will no longer have to sign an additional form for each patient attesting to the fact that all of the medications and treatments they ordered were proper. That alone eliminates 11 million forms and frees up 200,000 hours of doctor time each year. And instead of holding frequent inspections to make sure procedures are being followed and all the paperwork is in order, HCFA will check to see how the patients are doing. They will publish the results to help consumers make informed choices. They will inspect laboratories more selectively, focusing on those with past problems, and they will stop wasting money regulating lab tests that are done by machines that rarely make mistakes.

Meat and Poultry

Every year, Americans consume over 43 billion pounds of beef, pork, and poultry—more than 160 pounds per person.[6] Ensuring that meat is safe for American families is an important governmental mission. For most of the last century, federal inspectors have carried out that mission by using the old "poke and sniff" system, in which an overworked cadre of U.S. Department of Agriculture inspectors physically checked 95 percent of all that meat, using their eyes, noses, and hands to try to detect any problems.

In July 1996, President Clinton announced the overhaul of USDA's meat and poultry inspection process. The new system is HACCP, the same scientific methods that are making seafood safe. The government sets the goals, but gives each company the flexibility to design a plan to meet them. It replaces a reliance on outdated procedures with new scientific testing that will keep diseases out of the food supply far better than the old inspections ever could. The new food safety system balances government regulation and industry responsibility. Industry will assume some costs for new equipment and technology, including its own scientific testing to ensure food safety, while USDA will conduct other testing and oversight to ensure that industry is meeting its food safety responsibility. These changes will add an estimated one-tenth of one cent to the cost of a pound of meat—and will save an estimated $1 billion to $4 billion a year in the cost of food-borne illnesses. That's not much of a price to pay for a system that will far better ensure the safety of our food supply.[7]

Consumer Products

The Consumer Product Safety Commission is a government agency that touches virtually every American. It ensures that nearly 15,000 consumer goods under its jurisdiction do not pose undue risks to their users. Under Chairperson Ann Brown, the CPSC is a model of partnership with industry to achieve goals. Working with industry, the agency has developed over 300 voluntary standards, while promulgating only 50 mandatory, traditional rules—a six-to-one ratio. This approach yields results faster, and at less cost. For example, in April 1994, the CPSC presented information to manufacturers of children's clothing that drawstrings on jackets, coats, and sweatshirts posed a significant risk and were, in fact, killing children. Working with industry, the CPSC crafted a voluntary agreement to remove the dangerous drawstrings from most of the 20 million children's garments manufactured annually in the United States, without having to issue any new regulations. The problem was addressed in the span of four months—less time than it would have taken even to draft typical government regulations.

Similarly, the CPSC worked with manufacturers to address the hazard that window blind and drapery cords posed to small children. Since 1981, over 140 children between the ages of eight months and four years had died after being caught on such cords. When she took over the CPSC, Chairperson Brown saw the need to deal with this tragic situation. Working together, the agency and industry devised a program to eliminate the hazard. This was accomplished in six months and, again, without going through the expensive and time-consuming regulatory process. Most importantly, it will save children's lives.

Drug Interdiction

One of the latest alliances between business and government is the Business Anti-Smuggling Coalition, which started last August in San Diego and is spreading to other ports. Led by Mattel, Inc., in cooperation with the Customs Service, the Coalition is stopping drug smugglers from using shipments of toys and other goods from overseas. It is purely voluntary, but Mattel executives are having no problem recruiting dozens of other patriotic business leaders to join the alliance.

Helping Our Partners

The U.S. Business Advisor gives business one electronic stop to all the agencies that deal with business.[8] The Advisor was designed the way a commercial software product would be. Originally shown as an "alpha product" by President Clinton at the White House Conference on Small Business in 1995, with the President's direction it was designed and redesigned based on user groups of business customers.

These users from big and small businesses around the country worked with the product and told us what to change. They loved the idea of one electronic stop, but wanted to change just about everything else. So we did. A central theme in their thinking was that government is drowning them in information—they said "make it easy to find what we need and then let us do business." They wanted the ability to make transactions, such as applying for permits, or to find out how to solve problems, like getting rid of a health hazard.

The new Advisor, released this past spring, lets business search 106,000 federal World Wide Web addresses for information by typing in simple English queries, like "show me the regulations for cutting Christmas trees on federal lands." The President typed that in, and the Advisor answered. Results are returned in seconds, with a key passage highlighted.

The Advisor provides several ways to quickly reach agency home pages that are critical to business. The SBA's home page is often mentioned as one of the Web's most popular and is always adding new, "cool" stuff. Responding to business's requests for on-line transactions, SBA just put their fast-track loan applications on-line to be filled out and submitted without paper. Another Advisor link takes business to the OSHA home page. Employers can get "how to" advice there. Do you think you need to get rid of asbestos in your building?

OSHA has an expert system that helps you decide if you have a problem and what to do about it. Similar electronic tools address cadmium, lead, and the hazards of work in confined spaces.

The Advisor is a modern, state-of-the-art, electronic one-stop shop. There are some shops made out of good old bricks and mortar, too. Houston's U.S. General Store for Small Business dispenses nearly any service or information that a small business owner needs from the federal government in one place—with local government there, too. So far, the General Store has had about 4,000 customers. An independent survey says they love it. One customer, Roy Owens, got help with a loan, tax advice, and even contract leads with the Post Office. Roy says he has more work than he can handle, and he'll "go anywhere, any time to tell anybody that the store is the best thing he's ever seen from government." Business owners can get the same kind of one-stop service at the U.S. General Stores and SBA's "one-stop capital shops" in Atlanta, Kansas City, Philadelphia, and Boston.

EPA is making it easier for businesses to comply with environmental regulations. EPA has funded Small Business Compliance Assistance Centers for the metal finishing, printing, automotive repair, and farming industries to help these small businesses identify—in plain English—low-cost compliance and pollution prevention strategies. EPA also waives or reduces penalties for first-time violators if the business corrects the problem or comes into compliance with the law. And to top it all off, EPA is simplifying more than 70 percent of its regulations on business and eliminating 1,400 pages of obsolete rules.

There are also 88 U.S. Export Assistance Centers where companies that want to sell goods overseas can receive the collective assistance of staff from Commerce, the Small Business Administration, the Export-Import Bank, and state and local agencies. These centers and the 1-800-USA-TRADE number place all government export assistance resources at anybody's fingertips.

The Treasury, Labor Department, and Social Security Administration have teamed up with state and local governments and private organizations to reduce the paperwork burden of reporting and depositing payroll taxes by the nation's 6.2 million employers. Reports will only have to be filed with one agency, which will distribute the information to all federal, state, and local agencies that need it. This goes for withholding and reporting income tax, social security, unemployment insurance, and Medicare information. There is even an electronic version in the works that will be on the Internet. Federal tax deposits are now being made electronically too. The law says 1,500 big businesses must deposit payroll taxes electronically, but IRS made it so easy that 64,000 more companies do it voluntarily.

The biggest assistance that many small businesses need in order to get off the ground, or to expand, is a loan. The SBA has cut way, way back on the amount of paperwork and time it takes small entrepreneurs to obtain the backing they need. SBA has also boosted the amount of private capital available. The results speak for themselves: SBA arranged 55,000 small business loans last year, more than twice the number for 1992, for a total of $7.8 billion—a real shot in the arm for small business and the economy.

Who's the Enemy?

Some of the new partnerships are going so well that, frankly, it is a little embarrassing. 3M just nominated EPA for an award, for goodness sake.[9] The international trade community in Miami named Customs Commissioner George Weise their "Man of the Year." As Tommy Roland said, some people might think we're not doing our job because we're not hassling everybody anymore.

Well, hassling never was our job, and corporate America never was the enemy. The enemy is pollution, contaminated food, workplace and product hazards, and the small percentage of people who smuggle drugs, cheat on taxes, and deliberately pollute our environment. Our job is to stop all of them, and we are doing it better than ever—along with new partners eager to help get the job done.

SECRET FOUR: GOVERNMENT IS PARTNERING WITH COMMUNITIES

"And there's something else we can do together. We can reinvent government. We can switch from red tape to results. We can put the days of almighty, holier-than-thou, mister-know-it-all Washington behind us. We can become partners."

—— VICE PRESIDENT AL GORE,
REMARKS TO U.S. CONFERENCE OF MAYORS,
AUSTIN, TEXAS, JULY 23, 1995

"Clinton and Gore are trying to change this huge bureaucracy. It's like climbing a three-mile-high mountain, and they've made it to mile post one. Nobody's ever gotten to the one-mile post before. But there's still a long way to go." So says a big city leader with a national reputation for straight talk—a successful city government reinventor, Philadelphia's mayor, Ed Rendell.

"Most of our dealings with the federal government are with HUD" (Housing and Urban Development), Rendell explains. "HUD would get an A+ from me, across the board. Henry Cisneros is a *great* Secretary of HUD—he's the embodiment of the Administration's policy to cut regulations and red tape, and to give local government the maximum amount of flexibility to use money most effectively."[1]

"Empowerment Zones are an example," says Rendell. Philadelphia and neighboring Camden, New Jersey, share one of 105 new flexible federal grants to revitalize both urban and rural communities. These communities were chosen from over 500 applicants, based on the strength of their strategic plans and community partnerships.

Grants of up to $100 million, along with tax breaks to attract new businesses, go to "Empowerment Zones" in six big cities and three rural areas; two more cities received grants of over $100 million without tax incentives. There are smaller grants and tax breaks for 94 other areas (64 urban, 30 rural) called "Enterprise Communities." All told, Washington is providing more than $1.5 billion in flexible grants and more than $2.5 billion in tax incentives. The communities also receive special assistance in removing red tape and regulatory barriers that prevent the innovative uses of federal funds.[2]

Deciding how to revitalize the community and get the most for their money was a grassroots effort. To qualify, the community residents themselves, with help from city and county governments and local businesses, drew up plans to solve what they, not Washington, saw as their biggest problems. Most communities that got grants need more businesses, more jobs, and better low-cost housing, and they plan to stimulate all of that not with handouts, but with low-cost loans so the money will be replenished.

Rendell continues: "The Empowerment Zone really lets the people in the communities take control and be responsible for the outcome. But that was kind of easy for HUD to implement without lots of red tape, because the law itself had the right spirit. I'm more impressed with things like HUD's housing regulations. They've gotten rid of some of the most onerous, inflexible requirements on cities, like the 'one-for-one' rule on public housing. That rule said that if we tore down an abandoned high rise that had 580 units, we had to construct 580 new units, even though there hadn't been anybody living in there for five years. It was the same thing with single units. You can go to some blocks in Philadelphia where everybody's done a great job with their houses—put money into rehabilitating their houses—and right in the middle of the block there are two HUD scattered housing units that are *terrible*—places for drug dealing, places where kids got into trouble, a big negative on the neighborhood. But in the past, we couldn't demolish them without plans to build two new ones. So they'd sit there without ever being demolished or rehabilitated, doing nobody any good. HUD's shown the common sense to eliminate that rule. So we've brought down a number of high-rises and scattered units." Philadelphia is not the only city that has been able to get rid of those high-rise nightmares. In the past few years, 30,000 units have been razed, more than in the previous 12 years. And President Clinton recently set a goal to tear down another 70,000 in the next four years—a total of 100,000 urban eyesores gone.

Tearing down houses is not the ultimate goal. HUD has also created National Partners in Homeownership, comprising 58 national organizations representing lenders, real estate professionals, home builders, non-profit housing providers, and federal, state, and local governments. The goal is to achieve an all-time high rate of homeownership—67 percent of all American households by the end of the year 2000, creating up to eight million additional homeowners. The partners are making headway. By the spring of 1996, the national home-ownership rate was 65.1 percent, up from 64.2 percent at the end of 1994 (an increase of more than 1.5 million households). This is the highest rate since 1981, and the sharpest year-to-year increase in over three decades.

"HUD's made a wonderful change," according to Mayor Rendell. "And it's the same story on money for economic development. They've given us all kinds of flexibility to use that money most effectively. It's a night and day difference from the old way. They've done an excellent job. They haven't gotten rid of *all* the regs and *all* the burdens, but they've gotten rid of a tremendous share of them."

What about getting rid of all of them? Would the mayor welcome the kind of complete freedom some in Congress advocate in the form of block grants? "It's not freedom, it's baloney," says Rendell. "First of all, freedom from federal rules would have to be passed along to us by the state. And the state government is, if anything, less sympathetic to the cities than the feds are. So we'd never see all that freedom.

"But the main thing is that even if we got freedom from rules and red tape, we could only operate maybe 10 or 15 percent cheaper. They're talking about 25 percent cuts. You might be able to be just as effective if you had freedom and 10 percent less money. But no way are you going to be effective with 25 percent less. No way."

Rendell moved on to discuss the Environmental Protection Agency. "Under prior administrations, EPA was the single worst bureaucracy, promulgating regulations that avoided risks of one-in-a-trillion and had huge price tags to local governments. They've gone from that absurd starting point to...fair. For example, there's a scrap dealer here who handles old refrigerators. An EPA regulation says that you have to put a red tag on them certifying the safe disposal of freon. He employs a ton of people in jobs that pay $20 an hour, and they were about to fine him more than a million dollars, which would put him completely out of business, because he didn't have the tags right.[3] We argued it with them at the local level, the regional level, even the Washington level. I think we got it worked out, but they were going to put our guy out of business.

"But on the plus side, EPA's Brownfields effort makes a lot of sense," Rendell says. The Brownfields program is EPA's new way of getting abandoned industrial sites cleaned up and put back into the economy. The first success was in Cleveland, Ohio, at a 20-acre eyesore owned by Sunarhauserman, Inc. It had been sitting in Superfund limbo land for years, with prospective buyers and developers afraid to touch it, not so much because of the actual pollution but because the clean-up liability was unlimited. Now it is being cleaned up and houses four new businesses that contribute 180 new jobs and $1 million to the local tax base.[4] One of the latest Brownfields projects is right inside Philadelphia's American Street Empowerment Zone. EPA has agreed that the site of a small, abandoned gasoline tank farm can be sealed, paved over, and developed by businesses that are attracted by the Empowerment Zone's tax incentives and low-cost loans.

Here is a recent example from the West Coast: The creosote-soaked site of the Wyckoff Company's wood treatment plant on Seattle's waterfront is about to become a world-class port facility for American President Lines. If EPA had not become a partner, the 1,000 jobs that are coming would have gone south—literally—and the land would have lain there oozing poison into the harbor while the lawyers wrangled in court for years. But EPA and the Port of Seattle worked out a common-sense deal that is good for everybody.

"Look, there's clearly plenty of work to do yet—two more miles of mountain to climb," says Rendell, going back to his original metaphor. "But things are sure headed in the right direction."

Cities, Counties, States—Partners

Each year, the federal government attaches strings to nearly a quarter of a trillion dollars and gives it to state and local governments.[5] The strings that are attached make the state and local governments go through strange motions that frustrate citizens and state and local governments alike.

Tillamook County, Oregon, is on the end of some of those strings. The head of their health department, Sue Cameron, gives some good examples of the motions they go through. "We get federal money to immunize kids. That's a great idea, but it's not that simple. There are six different kinds of federal immunization money. One kind is for diphtheria. Another is for hepatitis-B, but only for teenagers. There's a different one for hepatitis-B for infants. Not a different shot—just different money. But that's not all. For the best protection, babies should get their first shots within two weeks of the day they're born, and most babies are born in hospitals. So, common sense tells you to have the hospital nurses give the shot while the babies are there. But before President Clinton launched the 'Vaccine for Children' program, the shots had to be given in public or private health clinics. That rule had kept some babies from ever getting their shots.

"And the bookkeeping! With each different kind of money for each different kind of thing—not just the different kinds of immunization, but nutrition programs, mental health, teen pregnancy, and so on—we have to keep separate records. That means that everybody who works here—from the receptionist to the doctor—is keeping track of which federal program they work on each minute to fill out time sheets for Washington."

Ask around Washington about all that red tape and it becomes clear that all the programs and all the rules are based on good intentions. All the strings were attached for good reasons. This is true; everybody in Washington is trying to achieve good government. But, as Gandhi said, "Good government is no substitute for self government." Somehow, we have to give government back to the people.

So how about having the feds cut all the strings and just hand money over in block grants? Mayor Rendell said the result would be too little freedom and way too little money. Here is what another potential recipient of block grants says. He is Jono Hildner, and he is the essence of Oregon—tall, fit, and outdoorsy, he runs wild rivers for fun. He also runs everything from public housing to the dog pound in Clackamas County, Oregon. Never heard of Clackamas County? In the 1800s it was the end of the Oregon Trail. Today, it is the beginning of Christmas—the nation's most prolific producer of Christmas trees. "Block grants are tempting," Jono says, "but I don't think the feds should just leave the money on a stump for us. I've seen that tried before. The money disappears and you're never sure what you got for it."

The Oregon Option

So where is the happy medium? We do not want all these Washington rules anymore. But we do want to make sure we get good results for all that money. Well, Sue Cameron and Jono Hildner are up to their necks in the happy medium right now in something called a "performance partnership."

In Oregon, the partnership is known as the "Oregon Option," and it is the wave of the future.[6] In December 1994, Oregon's Governor and numerous mayors and county commissioners signed an agreement with Vice President Gore and seven Cabinet Secretaries. They agreed to pilot a redesigned system that is:

- structured, managed, and evaluated on the basis of results;
- oriented to customer needs and satisfaction;
- biased toward preventing problems, not just fixing them afterward; and

- simplified and integrated as much as possible, dele-
gating responsibilities for service design, delivery,
and results to front-line, local-level providers.

Government reinventors believe in the adage, "Lead,
follow, or get out of the way." In the Oregon Option,
we are following. Through surveys in the early nineties,
the people of Oregon sorted out which issues were
most important to them—like cleaning up rivers,
increasing adult literacy, and reducing teen pregnancy.
They also set some performance goals—like going in
three years from 18 pregnant teens in a thousand to
only 10. They called the goals "Oregon Benchmarks."[7]
And they started tearing down the old-fashioned state
and local bureaucracy that stood in their way. In 1994,
they invited the feds to join them—to follow their
lead. We followed proudly.

"The feds don't make us fill out those stupid time
sheets anymore," says Sue Cameron. "And the seven
different immunization funds have been consolidated."
Jono Hildner adds, "The biggest improvement is communication. I've got somebody in Washington who
knows me now, who I can talk to, who understands our
problems and helps us get them fixed. I think the feds
should be doing a lot more of this."

Performance Partnerships

We agree, Jono. Based on the success of the Oregon Option, President Clinton has asked Congress to combine 271 separate grants and programs, which now have lots of strings attached, into 27 performance partnerships that are focused on results, just like Oregon's benchmarks. Each of the President's performance partnership grants would consolidate funding streams, eliminate overlapping authorities, create financial incentives to reward results, and reduce micromanagement and wasteful paperwork. So far, Congress has approved performance partnerships for rural development and the environment. The recently enacted Farm Bill created three new rural development performance partnerships in which a large number of programs—for rural utilities, economic development, and housing—will be administered together flexibly, with input on local needs from state and local officials, and focused on results.[8]

We are eager for Congress to complete its work in other areas where the President has proposed performance partnerships, and we and the states are ready to move as soon as Congress does. The Department of Health and Human Services, for example, has met with over 1,000 folks around the country—from states, localities, and consumer groups—to identify the public health results we all want and how best to measure progress. We also have partnerships with states and cities everywhere we could think of, in every way the current laws allow.

President Clinton has established a Community Empowerment Board of the major federal domestic agencies to support community-driven economic revitalization. The board helps break down the bureaucratic walls that sometimes keep agencies from responding effectively to state and local partners. The President has directed agencies to eliminate unnecessary regulatory and legal impediments. We are moving control and responsibility back to the people—providing top-down support for bottom-up reform.

The Environment

"These partnerships are based on a shared vision of environmental protection that is based on trust, respect, and a commitment to changing the way we do business. These grants are one of the top 25 [environmental] initiatives for reinventing government that President Clinton announced last March 17 [1995]"

—ADMINISTRATOR CAROL BROWNER[9]

Last May, EPA signed the first performance partnership grant agreements with Colorado and Utah. Through negotiation, EPA and states agree upon broad goals and priorities to achieve better environmental outcomes. The new, one-step grants replace up to 16 separate agreements the states used to have to negotiate and allow the states to shift money as priorities change, without time-consuming appeals to EPA. Gone are the 16 separate reports; there is just one report under the partnership grant. It is just the kind of change in government that we envisioned in the title of the first National Performance Review report: "From Red Tape to Results."

EPA is creating partnerships at the local level, too. When EPA became involved at a potential Superfund cleanup site in north Boulder, Colorado, several parties were entrenched in litigation about groundwater contamination. First, EPA informed the parties as to the potential risks involved in the status quo and then gave the community a chance to develop a solution before EPA put it on the Superfund list. Next, EPA invited all parties—including citizens—to accept some responsibility for resolving the disputes and cleaning up the water. Within six months, they had come up with a solution and a way to pay for it locally. This approach saved millions in federal dollars—and saved the community from being immersed in the Superfund program for the next decade.

EPA, Energy, and other federal agencies, along with 22 state environmental agencies, have pioneered a successful partnering effort to improve the cleanup process for contaminated toxic sites. Together, these groups break down the barriers to using innovative environmental technologies for remediation and treatment of hazardous and radioactive wastes. Partnering has streamlined the regulatory process for environmental technologies and moved states and federal agencies toward results-oriented cleanup.

The Bureau of Land Management has created 24 resource advisory councils in the Western states to advise the Bureau on issues concerning management of the public's lands and resources. These councils, developed under the Federal Advisory Committee Act, are made up of 12 to 15 members appointed by the Secretary of the Interior from among individuals nominated by the public and state governors. Three groups are represented on these councils: business; conservationists; and local citizens, including representatives of local government and Indian tribes. The councils have been very successful at bringing diverse—and often competing—interests to the table to deal with each other on issues of mutual concern. The approach shows great promise in successfully solving long-standing problems of public land management. Many individuals who were initially skeptical of the councils are now quite supportive of their work and are optimistic that they will be a strong force in resolving disputes about the uses of public land in the West.

Connecticut Neighborhood Revitalization Partnership

In 1995, Connecticut passed an innovative law, the Neighborhood Revitalization Act, which requires the state and its municipalities to break down barriers in response to neighborhoods' comprehensive plans and measurable goals to revitalize their economies and neighborhoods. In 1996, the federal government joined the party. This partnership allows federal barriers to be overcome along with state barriers and allows federal, state, and local partners to work together to improve Connecticut's poorest communities through economic development and neighborhood revitalization. The Neighborhood Revitalization Zone process invites residents, businesses, and municipal officials to develop a strategic plan to revitalize their neighborhood. Grassroots planning and community organizing are the key components of this concept, just as in the Oregon Option, Empowerment Zones, and Enterprise Communities.

Addressing Unfunded Mandates

The Clinton-Gore Administration fully understands the burdens states and localities face when the federal government imposes mandates without providing adequate funding. In October 1993, President Clinton signed the first executive order requiring all federal agencies to consult with state and local organizations before promulgating any rules or regulations that impose new unfunded mandates.[10]

In March 1995, President Clinton signed the Unfunded Mandates Reform Act, which restricts the ability of Congress to impose costly mandates on states, localities, and tribal governments.[11] Based on analyses required by the Congressional Budget Office, mandates costing states and localities $50 million or more in any of the first five years after becoming effective are not permitted—unless waived by majority votes in both the House and Senate. The Act also requires greater intergovernmental consultations in the administrative rule-making process and allowance for the least expensive means of complying with federal regulations.

Welfare and Health Care Reform

One of the best pieces of evidence that Washington is changing its ways—becoming a partner with communities instead of a know-it-all—is its willingness to clear the way for welfare reform. We all have the same goal, to make welfare a hand-up to a decent life, instead of a hand-out for life. But there are different ways to get there. While Congress was debating the different ways over the past few years, the President let states try them to see what worked best. The Clinton Administration has approved welfare demonstration projects in more than 40 states—twice as many as the previous two administrations combined.

The new, national welfare reform legislation incorporates many of the good ideas being tried by the states. The Indiana welfare reform plan, which is typical of the scores of demonstration projects approved by the Clinton Administration, puts 12,000 able-bodied welfare recipients on a "placement track" where they get special help finding a job—including subsidies for employers. Parents have to keep their kids in school and get them immunized. Adults receive up to two years of special help finding a job, then their welfare benefits run out. Children's benefits continue, but there are no new benefits for additional children conceived on welfare. The President approved Indiana's plan in late 1994, and between March of 1995 and March of 1996, Indiana's welfare rolls dropped by 22 percent.[12]

President Clinton has done the same thing for states wanting to try health care reforms. Tennessee, for example, can now expand health care coverage to over 400,000 people who were previously uninsured. To date, the President has approved 13 comprehensive health care reform demonstrations similar to Tennessee's—working in partnership with states to increase the use of managed care, improve the quality of care, and expand coverage to 2.2 million low-income uninsured Americans.

These are not Washington's latest bright ideas being imposed on communities. They are ideas from the communities themselves—from the people who understand the problems best and who will live with the results. To be fair, Washington does have some experts with a wealth of experience to share and, of course, the financial resources that communities need. But now, communities don't have to follow Washington's rules to get Washington's money. It is the people's money and Washington is becoming the people's partner.

Fighting Crime

Some of our partnerships are making America's streets safer. Legislation that President Clinton fought for is putting 100,000 community police on the streets, and crime in our cities is now at its lowest rate in years. But fighting crime is more than just a matter of brute force. The Justice Department has teamed up with state and local police on an innovation that really works.[13] It is called, appropriately enough, COPS, for Community Oriented Policing Services. Just look what it did for Tampa, Florida: A few years ago, Tampa had a tough crime problem.[14] Then, with a $3.8 million partnership grant from the Department of Justice, a 15-officer COPS squad joined forces with the local police and made a 23 percent dent in every crime category, with drug busts up by 51 percent.[15]

How? First, COPS got out of the patrol cars and mixed in with the community. The Tampa COPS immediately investigate crimes themselves, instead of relaying the information and responsibility to detectives. COPS keep kids in school and off the streets, a tactic that has drastically reduced crime during school hours. COPS hold auctions where kids bid community service hours in exchange for impounded, unclaimed bicycles. COPS organized the area's first Girl Scout troop, and they are starting a Boy Scout troop. COPS organized crime watch groups made up of volunteers who canvass their communities and help eliminate crimes such as vandalism, street-drinking, curfew violations, and prostitution. For every COPS officer in the community, there are dozens of watchful citizens who take pride in the cleanliness and safety of their community. This is government in partnership with the people.

Another crime-fighting partnership, Operation Safe Home, teams local and state law enforcement with the resources of HUD, Justice, Treasury, and the Office of National Drug Control Policy. This innovative partnership has not only combated gangs, drugs, and violence, but has also brought together a range of crime prevention initiatives to ensure long-term safety. Since 1994, Operation Safe Home has made a nationwide improvement in the safety of public housing with results like 8,000 arrests and the confiscation of 1,000 weapons as well as $5 million in drugs and drug money.[16]

Education

*"Over the last two years, the Congress and the
U.S. Department of Education have made tremendous
progress in transforming the federal relationship*

> *with the states on education. It has changed from one*
> *based on regulatory compliance to one based on*
> *accountability and performance."*

— ROBERT V. ANTONUCCI,
MASSACHUSETTS COMMISSIONER OF EDUCATION[17]

Some of the most impressive examples of the way government is changing to partnership are in the Department of Education. In Goals 2000, the Education Department led states to set challenging academic standards for their students, and then the reinvented Department of Education let them get to work.[18] States no longer have to submit their plans to the experts in Washington for approval; they just need to *have* a plan, a schedule for progress, and a way to measure progress. And they don't have to report their progress to Washington, either; they report it to the people. If selected federal laws or regulations stand in the way of progress, the Secretary of Education has the authority to waive them—he has waived more than 100 already.

States that really want to get on board—those willing to waive their own rules and let local school districts be accountable—can waive federal rules without even asking Washington for permission. The program is called Ed-Flex. The measure of success is simple: improved academic performance of the students. Eight states have signed up and there is room for four more; the legal limit is 12, for now. [19]

THE NATIONAL EDUCATION GOALS

By the Year 2000:

- All children in America will start school ready to learn.
- The high school graduation rate will increase to at least 90 percent.
- All students will leave grades 4, 8, and 12 having demonstrated competency over challenging subject matter in the core academic subjects.
- U.S. students will be first in the world in mathematics and science achievement.
- Every adult American will be literate and will possess the knowledge and skills necessary to compete in a global economy and exercise the rights and responsibilities of citizenship.
- Every school in the U.S. will be free of drugs, violence, and the unauthorized presence of fire-arms and alcohol and will offer a disciplined environment conducive to learning.

- The nation's teaching force will have access to programs for the continued improvement of their professional skills and the opportunity to acquire the knowledge and skills needed to instruct and prepare all American students for the next century.
- Every school will promote partnerships that will increase parental involvement and participation in promoting the social, emotional, and academic growth of children.

Since the goal of all this academic freedom is better academic performance, let's look at some results. Maryland, one of the Ed-Flex states, reports a 52 percent leap in the number of schools whose students are doing well at the third grade level. They are up by 13 percent at the fifth grade level and by 32 percent at the eighth grade. Forty percent of all students statewide met the state standards—that's a 25 percent gain over 1993.[20]

It is no surprise that flexibility, local control, and measured accountability produce good results. Kentucky has been doing it since 1990 with great success, and we copied the idea from them. Kentucky schools manage themselves through councils that include teachers, parents, and community members. They set goals and measure success by looking at things like student test scores, dropout rates, success at getting jobs, and how many students go on to college. Schools that make their goals get bonuses that school staffs decide how to spend. Schools that do not make the grade get special help from the state.

Results? Grades have been going up steadily the last two years, especially for fourth, eighth, and twelfth graders. The fourth graders were best of all—their grades went up about 10 percentage points overall, and a whopping 16 percentage points in reading.[21] Way to go, fourth graders! Way to go, Kentucky!

From teaching kids how to read to fighting crime in the streets, from big cities like Philadelphia to rural counties like Tillamook, from both coasts and places in between, people in governments closest to the people are seeing the change for the better. The National Performance Review is leading the shift away from Washington's well-intentioned efforts at good government toward the grassroots power of self-government. Ed Rendell is right—we are at the one-mile post of a three-mile mountain. Let's get a good grip and keep climbing.

CONCLUSION

I haven't tried to compile an exhaustive list of all the problems the President and I have faced trying to reinvent government, or of all the successes we've scored—there just aren't enough pages in an easy-to-read book to be fair to all the hard-working government reinventors that are helping us. If you'd like an even more complete story about how the federal government is getting its act together, turn on a computer and call up our World Wide Web site.[1] There are hundreds of success stories there.

The point of this short book is just to show you that we "get it"—President Clinton and I understand what's wrong with how the government has been doing things—and we are turning things around. The battle against the old forces of big government, central control, and mistrust isn't won yet, but everything is moving in the right direction. And, we have a plan to continue the changes.

First, we are turning some of today's agencies into smaller, sleeker organizations that won't look like government at all. They will be like private companies, with a real CEO on contract to cut costs, and a free hand when it comes to the remaining government rules about procurement, personnel, and the like. The British government did this a few years ago, and costs have been dropping steadily. We'll borrow their good idea.

On customer service, we'll stick our necks out even further. The top boss of every agency that touches millions of Americans—like the IRS and VA and Customs—is on the line to make dramatic improvements in service this year. There's even a Web page where you can read their specific goals and let them know what you think.[2]

Regulatory agencies are on orders to make partnership with businesses their standard way of operating. We have tested it long enough to know it increases compliance with the laws of the land. After all, compliance is what we're after—not meaningless hassles. Now we can move beyond pilot programs for partnership into the mainstream.

The same goes for federal grants to state and local governments. No more having to follow the federal rule books to receive federal funds. We will focus on results and consider replacing many grant programs with performance-based partnerships. And to dispel the last vestiges of nameless, faceless bureaucracy, we will give each of our community partners a single, live federal employee, complete with name and face, who will help them with any and all business in Washington, regardless of which agency's turf it is.

Finally, we are going to do better by our workforce. Any *Fortune* 500 company would be lucky to have a workforce like the federal government's. We need to invest in it: better tools and training, closer partnership between labor and management, more opportunities and challenges for our senior executives.

All of the progress we have made, and all of our plans for the future are focused on one goal—restoring the American people's faith in their own system of self-government—the people's belief that we can solve our national problems by working together through the institutions of self-government. Faith in government is at a low point, and that lack of faith threatens the nation's future. Government can't do everything, and it certainly shouldn't try. But some national problems like drugs, violence, poverty, and pollution can be solved only by Americans working together through our system of self-government. If we lose faith in that, we abandon the future to chaos.

Reinvention restores our faith. Americans find government service improving over the counter and over the phone. Business leaders find federal regulators ready to use common sense and to look for common ground.

Communities find the walls coming down between agencies and levels of government, and beyond the old walls they find partners ready to do whatever it takes to solve problems. Reinvention is securing the future of self-government in America.

So, if you see government changing, don't keep it a secret. Tell your friends, your business associates, your neighbors. Tell them government can do things right. I'm the first to admit that government isn't the answer to all our problems. But when government has to be part of the solution, more and more, we Americans can count on getting results.

AL GORE

NOTES

Introduction

1. The Postal Service is not included. It has grown because it has more mail to deliver, but it is financed primarily from the sale of stamps, not from taxes.

2. Unpublished calculation prepared by the Office of Management and Budget, based on civilian pay and benefits budgeted for fiscal year 1996.

3. Office of Management and Budget, *Budget for Fiscal Year 1997, Historical Tables,* "Table 1.1 - Summary of Receipts, Outlays, and Surpluses or Deficits: 1789-2002" (Washington, D.C.: Government Printing Office, 1996), p. 20.

4. Office of Personnel Management, Office of Workforce Information, Central Personnel Data File (unpublished data).

5. General Accounting Office, *Federal Downsizing: The Costs and Savings of Buyouts versus Reductions-In-Force* (Washington, D.C.: Government Printing Office), GAO/GGD-96-63, May 14, 1996.

6. Office of Personnel Management, Office of Workforce Information, Central Personnel Data File (unpublished data). This figure (114,856 buyouts) includes all civilian defense and non-defense personnel who took buyouts between January 1993 and January 1996.

7. Office of Personnel Management, Office of Workforce Information, Central Personnel Data File (unpublished

data). Between January 1993 and January 1996, 239,286 personnel left federal employment. Of these, 21,125 were separated involuntarily.

8. Stephen Barr, "A Simple Suggestion Worth Millions: Civil Servant's Idea Expected to Mean Big Savings in Procurements," *Washington Post*, October 13, 1994.

9. Vice President Al Gore, *Common Sense Government: Works Better and Costs Less* (New York: Random House, 1995), p. 26.

Secret One: Common Sense Has Come to the Federal Government

1. Unpublished data on drug seizure activity in passenger processing provided by U.S. Customs Service, Miami. The data include seizures as of July 31, 1996.

2. Unpublished data on FTS2000, the Federal Telecommunications System, from the General Services Administration.

3. General Accounting Office, *Acquisition: Purchase Card Use Cuts Procurement Costs, Improves Efficiency* (Washington, D.C.: Government Printing Office), GAO/NSIAD-96-138, August 6, 1996.

4. Public Law 104-106, *National Defense Authorization Act for FY 1996,* February 10, 1996; Executive Order 13011, *Federal Information Technology,* July 17, 1996.

5. Unpublished data from the Office of Management and Budget.

6. Letter from Peter J. Hannes, President, Special Markets Division, Jockey International, Inc. to Mr. Dennis Dudek, Department of Defense, June 7, 1996.

7. Department of Defense, Office of Assistant Secretary (Public Affairs), "Defense Acquisition Pilot Programs Forecast Cost/Schedule Savings of Up to 50 Percent From Acquisition Reform," News Release No. 138-96, March 14, 1996; and unpublished data provided by the Department of Defense.

8. See Presidential Memorandum, *Streamlining Procurement Through Electronic Commerce,* October 26, 1993; Executive Order 12931, *Federal Procurement Reform,* October 13, 1994; Executive Order 12979, *Agency Procurement Protests,* October 25, 1995; and Executive Order 13011, *Federal Information Technology,* July 17, 1996.

9. Unpublished data from the Federal Communications Commission.

10. Al Gore, *Creating a Government That Works Better & Costs Less* (Washington, D.C.: Government Printing Office, September 7, 1993), pp. 13-14.

11. James Thompson, "The Reinvention Revolution," *Government Executive,* Vol. 28, No. 5, May 1996, pp. 39-41. See also, General Accounting Office, *Management Reform: Status of Agency Reinvention Lab Efforts,* (Washington, D.C.: Government Printing Office) GAO-GGD-96-69, March 20, 1996.

12. President and Mrs. Harrison were afraid to touch the light switches, so a civil servant was assigned to switch the lights on in the evening, let them burn all night, and return in the morning to switch them off. James Trager, *The People's Chronology* (New York: Henry Holt and Company, Inc., 1996), pp. 561, 572, 587.

13. Congressional Testimony by James King, Director, Office of Personnel Management, before the House Committee on Government Reform and Oversight, October 12, 1995.

14. Each agency now has the authority to do its own hiring (Public Law 104-52), but many agencies choose to hire through the Office of Personnel Management's phone-in center.

15. Executive Order 12871, *Labor-Management Partnerships,* October 1, 1993.

16. U. S. Mint, "Denver Mint Receives National Partnership Award for Improved Labor-Management Relations," Press Release, February 14, 1996.

17. Presidential Memorandum, *Expanding Family-Friendly Work Arrangements in the Executive Branch,* July 11, 1994; Presidential Memorandum, *Supporting the Role of Fathers in Families,* June 16, 1995; and Presidential Memorandum, *Implementing Family-Friendly Work Arrangements,* June 21, 1996.

18. Michael Serlin, "The Competitors," *Government Executive,* Vol. 28, No. 6, June 1996, pp. 29-33.

Secret Two: Government Is Serving People Better

1. Undated letter from Robert J. Lacombe to Shirley Chater, Commissioner, Social Security Administration.

2. Letter from Lloyd Hartford regarding the Dedicated Commuter Lane Project, April 12, 1996.

3. Anonymous comment sheet from the Dedicated Commuter Lane.

4. Letter from Chris Petersen to the Department of Energy, Energy Information Administration.

5. Letter from Michael R. McMeekin to D. James Baker, Undersecretary for Oceans and Atmosphere, National Oceanic and Atmosphere Administration, May 6, 1996.

6. Undated letter from an unidentified police officer to Eljay B. Bowron, Director, United States Secret Service.

7. Undated letter from Alexander Schuster, veteran, to Director and Chief of Staff of a Veterans Affairs hospital.

8. Public Law 96-511, *Paperwork Reduction Act of 1980,* December 11, 1980, 94 Stat. 2813.

9. Bill Clinton and Al Gore, *Putting Customers First '95,* (Washington, D.C.: Government Printing Office), October 1995. The electronic version is located at "http://www.npr.gov".

10. Ibid., p. 123.

11. Postal Service, "It's a Record— 90 Percent On Time Delivery!" Press Release No. 49, Washington, D.C., June 4, 1996. The U.S. Postal Service's Internet address is "http://www.usps.gov".

12. President Clinton directed agencies in 1993 to appoint chief operating officers (normally the deputy secretary of the department or the head of the agency. He then convened two dozen of the chief operating officers of the departments and largest agencies as the President's Management Council to share their best practices and advise him on ways to implement reinvention.

13. Dalbar Financial Services, Inc., "Social Security Administration Tops in Customer Service," Press Release, Boston, Massachusetts, May 3, 1995.

14. Although the General Services Administration promised to have blue pages in five cities, seven cities have already signed up. They are: Baltimore, Chicago, Denver, Indianapolis, Los Angeles, New York, and San Francisco.

15. Unpublished calculation from the Office of Management and Budget.

16. PEBES stands for "Personal Earnings and Benefit Statement," and it is located at "http://www.ssa.gov".

17. Send your geology questions by e-mail to: "ask-a-geologist@usgs.gov".

18. The fax number for the Bureau of Labor Statistics' Fax on Demand is 202-606-6325.

19. The World Wide Web address for HUD's city maps is "http://www.hud.gov/communit.html".

20. The World Wide Web address for the Bond Wizard is "http://www.ustreas.gov/treasury/bureaus/pub-debt/savwizar/html".

21. Undated letter from the Bodde Family to the Federal Emergency Management Agency.

Secret Three: Government Is
in Partnership with Business

1. Bob Bauer, "A Swimming Time for Shrimp; Frozen Sales Up in 1994," *Supermarket News,* Vol. 44, No. 52, December 26, 1994.

2. Unpublished data provided by the Environmental Protection Agency.

3. Calculation based on unpublished data from the Environmental Protection Agency.

4. Unpublished data provided by the Environmental Protection Agency, Environmental Assistance Division.

5. Letter from Jack Cohen, Ph.D., Vice President for Quality & Compliance, Scios, Inc., to Gregory Bobrowicz, District Director, Food and Drug Administration, Alameda, CA, May 29, 1996.

6. U. S. Department of Agriculture, National Agricultural Statistics Service, "Livestock Slaughter 1995," March 1996.

7. Jerry Knight, "Meat Inspection Changes Produce an Unusual Unanimity," *Washington Post,* July 9, 1996, p. D1, citing Administrator Michael R. Taylor of the Food Safety and Inspection Service, U.S. Department of Agriculture.

8. The U.S. Business Advisor is located at "http://www.business.gov".

9. The EPA 33/50 team was nominated by 3M for Vice President Gore's Hammer Award and received the award in June 1996.

Secret Four: Government Is Partnering with Communities

1. To learn more about HUD partnerships with Philadelphia and other cities, visit the HUD homepage at "http://www.hud.gov".

2. Department of Housing and Urban Development, "Empowerment Zones and Enterprise Communities," *Community Connections*. To learn more about the Empowerment Zone/Enterprise Community initiative, visit the homepage at "http://www.ezec.gov".

3. EPA believed that some of the scrap refrigerators still contained freon, which could have escaped into the atmosphere; freon is harmful to the environment because it destroys ozone.

4. Environmental Protection Agency, "Removing Liability Barriers and Encouraging Development," unpublished information, June 20, 1996.

5. Office of Management and Budget, *FY 1997 President's Budget, Analytical Perspectives,* "Aid to State and Local Governments," March 1996, p. 167.

6. Memorandum of Understanding, "The Oregon Option," (unpublished) December 1994, p. 1.

7. Oregon Progress Board, "Oregon Benchmarks:

Standards for Measuring Statewide Progress and Institutional Performance," Report to the 1995 Legislature, December 1994.

8. Public Law 104-127, *Federal Agricultural Improvement and Reform Act of 1996,* April 4, 1996.

9. Environmental Protection Agency, "Environmental News," Press Release, Washington, D.C., May 16, 1996.

10. Executive Order 12871, *Enhancing the Intergovernmental Partnership,* October 1, 1993.

11. Public Law 104-4, Unfunded Mandates Reform Act of 1995, March 22, 1995.

12. Unpublished data from the Administration for Children and Families, Department of Health and Human Services.

13. Justice cut all the red tape associated with COPS. Communities need only fill out a one-page application.

14. Pam Noles, "No Tax Increases in New Budget," *The Tampa Tribune,* July 31, 1996, p. 1.

15. Unpublished information from the Department of Justice, June 21, 1996.

16. Nicole Marshall, "65 Arrested in Sweep of Public Housing," *Tulsa World,* May 31, 1996, p. A8.

17. Robert V. Antonucci, Massachusetts Commissioner of Education, The Federal Role in Education Reform, Testimony before House Subcommittee on Early Childhood, Youth and Families, House Committee on Economic and Education Opportunities, June 21, 1995.

18. Department of Education, *Goals 2000: Increasing Student Achievement Through State and Local Initiatives,* (Washington, D.C.: Government Printing Office) April 30, 1996.

19. The Ed-Flex states are: Kansas, Oregon, Massachusetts, Texas, Ohio, Vermont, Maryland, and Colorado.

20. Maryland State Department of Education, *High Expectations Producing Better Schools, State School Superintendent Grasmick Says,* Baltimore, MD: Press Release, December 12, 1995.

21. "1992–1994 Kentucky Accountability Results," *The Cincinnati Enquirer,* February 8, 1995, p. B2.

Conclusion

1. The National Performance Review homepage address is "http://www.npr.gov".

2. Customer service standards can be found at "http://www.info.gov/Info/html/customer_service.htm".

INDEX

ABOUT THE AUTHOR

Vice President AL GORE was a journalist for seven years before winning a seat in the House of Representatives in 1976. In 1984 he was elected to the Senate, and in 1992 he was chosen as Bill Clinton's running mate. The author of the best selling *Earth in the Balance: Ecology and the Human Spirit*, the Vice President lives in Washington, D.C., and Carthage, Tennessee, with his wife, Tipper, and their four children.